Master Google Workspace 2025

A Practical Productivity Manual: Learn All G Suite
Tools for Faster Workflows and Better Collaboration

Marcus D. Rye

Table of content

INTRODUCTION

The way we work has undergone a dramatic transformation. Remote work, digital collaboration, and cloud computing have become the norm rather than the exception. Amid this technological shift, Google Workspace 2025 offers a comprehensive suite of tools designed to enhance productivity and streamline workflows for individuals and organizations.

Google Workspace 2025, formerly known as G Suite, is a cloud-based productivity suite that brings together essential tools like Gmail, Google Drive, Google Docs, Google Sheets, Google Slides, Google Calendar, and many more under one cohesive platform. Now small business owners looking to streamline business operations, teachers looking to create engaging online lessons, and professionals aiming to enhance office workflow, can achieve higher levels of productivity using Google Workspace 2025 tools.

What makes Google Workspace 2025 stand out is its ability to seamlessly integrate various applications, enabling real-time collaboration and communication. Imagine working on a document with colleagues located across the globe, making edits simultaneously, and discussing changes via video conference—all within the same platform. This level of integration and ease of use not only boosts productivity but also fosters a collaborative spirit that is essential in today's work environment.

This book is designed to be your comprehensive guide to mastering Google Workspace. We will explore each tool in detail, providing step-by-step instructions, practical tips, and real-world examples to help you get the most out of these powerful applications. From setting up your Google Workspace account to leveraging advanced features for project management, this guide will equip you with the knowledge and skills to navigate and utilize Google Workspace effectively.

This guide is for anyone looking to make the most out of Google Workspace. Whether you're tech-savvy or just starting to explore digital tools, this book will help you navigate through the complexities with ease.

The content withing these pages are structured to take you from the basics of setting up your Google Workspace account to mastering the advanced features. Each section is designed to build on the previous one, ensuring you gain a comprehensive understanding of each tool and how it can benefit you. We'll provide detailed, step-by-step instructions for setting up and using each tool. This approach ensures you won't miss any crucial steps and can follow along at your own pace.

Along the way, we'll share valuable tips and tricks to help you work more efficiently and make the most of the features available in Google Workspace. Real-world examples will be provided to demonstrate how you can apply what you've learned to your own situation. This will help you see the practical benefits of each tool and how it can solve common problems.

How to Set Up Your Google Workspace Account

Step 1: Go to the Google Workspace website and click the "Get Started" button. Enter your business name, number of employees, and current email address.

Step 2: Choose your domain. You can use an existing domain or purchase a new one through Google. This domain will be used for your business email addresses.

Step 3: Create your primary administrator account. This will be your main account for managing Google Workspace. Choose a secure username and password.

Step 4: Verify your domain. Google will provide a verification code or file to add to your website's hosting server. Follow the instructions to complete the verification.

Step 5: Add users to your account. In the Admin Console, go to the Users section and click "Add User." Enter the names and email addresses for your team members.

Step 6: Set up Gmail. Configure settings in the Admin Console, such as email forwarding and aliases, to streamline communication for your team.

Step 7: Set up Google Drive. Create shared drives for departments or projects and set permissions for who can view, edit, and share files.

Step 8: Explore other Google Workspace apps like Google Calendar, Google Meet, and Google Docs. Customize these tools to fit your business needs and enhance collaboration.

By following these steps, you'll have your Google Workspace account set up and ready to boost your team's productivity and collaboration.

Setting up a Google Admin Console

The Google Admin Console is the central hub for managing your Google Workspace account. As the administrator, you'll use this powerful tool to control user access, configure settings, and ensure the security of your organization's data. Let's break down the process of using the Google Admin Console step-by-step to help you manage your workspace effectively.

Step 1: Access the Admin Console. To get started, sign in to your Google Workspace account using your administrator credentials. Once logged in, click on the grid icon (Google Apps menu) in the upper right corner of the screen and select "Admin." This will take you to the Admin Console dashboard.

Step 2: Create a new user. In the Admin Console, navigate to the Users section. Here, you can add new users by clicking the "Add User" button. Enter the user's first and last name, and choose a username. Google will generate a temporary password for the new user, which they will need to change upon their first login. Creating user accounts allows your team members to access Google Workspace apps using your business domain.

Step 3: Edit user information. Managing user details is straightforward in the Admin Console. To update a user's information, go to the Users section, select the user you want to edit, and click on their name. You can update their profile information, reset passwords, and manage their account settings. Keeping user information up-to-date is crucial for smooth communication and collaboration within your organization.

Step 4: Suspend or delete a user. If an employee leaves your organization or no longer needs access to Google Workspace, you can suspend or delete their account. To do this, go to the Users section, select the user, and choose either "Suspend User" or "Delete User." Suspending an account temporarily disables access without deleting data, while deleting an account removes all user data and access permanently.

Step 5: Manage user roles. Assigning roles helps you delegate administrative responsibilities. In the Admin Console, go to the Users section, select the user, and click "Assign Roles." You can assign roles such as Super Admin, Group Admin, or Service Admin, each with different levels of access and control. This feature ensures that administrative tasks are distributed efficiently while maintaining security.

Step 6: Manage devices. The Admin Console allows you to oversee the devices connected to your Google Workspace account. Navigate to the Devices section to view and manage the list of devices. You can enforce security policies, monitor device activity, and wipe data from lost or stolen devices. This helps protect your organization's data and ensures compliance with security protocols.

Step 7: Manage apps. Controlling which apps are available to your users is essential for maintaining productivity and security. In the Admin Console, go to the Apps section. Here, you can enable or disable apps, manage app settings, and configure third-party app integrations. This allows you to customize the app experience based on your organization's needs.

Step 8: Configure security settings. Security is a top priority for any organization. In the Admin Console, navigate to the Security section to configure settings such as two-factor authentication, password policies, and account recovery options. Implementing robust security measures helps protect your organization's data from unauthorized access and potential threats.

Step 9: Access reporting and analytics. The Admin Console provides detailed reports and analytics to help you monitor usage and identify trends. Go to the Reports section to view data on user activity, app usage, and security events. These insights can inform your decision-making and help you optimize your Google Workspace environment.

Step 10: Utilize support and resources. Google provides extensive support and resources to help you manage your Google Workspace account. In the Admin Console, you can access help articles, community forums, and direct support from Google experts. Leveraging these resources ensures you have the assistance you need to resolve issues and maximize the benefits of Google Workspace.

How to Create a New User

Creating a new user in Google Workspace is a straightforward process that allows you to provide individual accounts for your employees or team members. These accounts will give them access to Google Workspace tools under your domain.

Step 1: Access the Google Admin Console. Start by signing in to your Google Workspace account with your administrator credentials. Once logged in, click on the grid icon (Google Apps menu) in the upper right corner and select "Admin" to open the Admin Console.

Step 2: Navigate to the Users section. In the Admin Console dashboard, find and click on the "Users" section. This is where you manage all the user accounts for your organization.

Step 3: Click on the "Add User" button. In the Users section, you'll see an option to "Add User" at the top of the page. Click on this button to start the process of creating a new user account.

Step 4: Enter the user's information. A form will appear where you need to input the new user's details. Fill in the first name, last name, and desired email address for the new user. This email address will be under your domain (e.g., user@yourcompany.com).

Step 5: Set a temporary password. Google will generate a temporary password for the new user. You can either let Google create one automatically or set a custom temporary password yourself. The new user will need to change this password upon their first login.

Step 6: Assign organizational unit. If you have different organizational units (OUs) set up within your Google Workspace, you can assign the new user to a specific OU. This helps in managing permissions and settings based on department or team. Select the appropriate organizational unit for the new user.

Step 7: Configure additional settings (optional). You have the option to configure additional settings, such as adding recovery information (phone number and alternate email), setting the user's location, or customizing their profile. These settings can enhance account security and help in user management.

Step 8: Save the new user. Once all the information is entered and reviewed, click the "Add" button to create the new user account. The user will receive an email with their login details and instructions on how to set up their account.

Step 9: Inform the new user. It's a good practice to personally inform the new user about their new Google Workspace account. Provide them with their username, temporary password, and a brief guide on how to log in and set up their account for the first time.

How to Edit your Information

Editing user information in Google Workspace is a straightforward process that allows you to keep user profiles up-to-date and manage account settings efficiently.

Step 1: Access the Google Admin Console. Start by logging into your Google Workspace account using your administrator credentials. Once logged in, click on the grid icon in the upper right corner to open the Google Apps menu, and select "Admin" to enter the Admin Console.

Step 2: Navigate to the Users section. In the Admin Console dashboard, locate and click on the "Users" section. This is where you can view and manage all user accounts within your organization.

Step 3: Select the user you want to edit. In the Users section, you'll see a list of all users. Find the user whose information you want to edit by scrolling through the list or using the search bar to locate them quickly. Click on the user's name to open their account details.

Step 4: Edit the user's profile information. Once you're in the user's account details, you'll see various fields such as name, email address, and contact information. Click on the field you want to edit, make the necessary changes, and then save your changes. For example, you might need to update a user's name if they've legally changed it or update their email address if they've moved to a different department.

Step 5: Update the user's organizational unit. If the user has moved to a different department or team within your organization, you can change their organizational unit. To do this, find the section labeled "Organizational Unit" and select the appropriate unit from the dropdown menu. This ensures the user has access to the correct resources and permissions.

Step 6: Adjust user settings. You can also update various user settings, such as password reset options, account recovery information, and security settings. For example, if a user forgets their password, you can reset it for them and provide a new temporary password.

Step 7: Review and save changes. After making all necessary edits to the user's information and settings, review your changes to ensure everything is correct. Once you're satisfied, click the "Save" button to apply the updates. The changes will take effect immediately.

Step 8: Inform the user of changes. It's good practice to notify the user of any significant changes to their account, especially if you've updated their email address, password, or organizational unit. This helps avoid any confusion and ensures they are aware of the updates.

Suspending or Deleting a User

Managing user accounts in Google Workspace involves not only creating and editing users but also knowing how to suspend or delete accounts when necessary. Whether an employee leaves the organization or you need to temporarily disable access.

Step 1: Access the Google Admin Console. Begin by logging into your Google Workspace account using your administrator credentials. Click on the grid icon in the upper right corner to open the Google Apps menu, then select "Admin" to enter the Admin Console.

Step 2: Navigate to the Users section. On the Admin Console dashboard, locate and click on the "Users" section. This area allows you to manage all user accounts within your organization.

Step 3: Select the user you want to suspend or delete. In the Users section, find the user account you wish to modify. You can scroll through the list or use the search bar to locate the specific user quickly. Click on the user's name to open their account details.

Step 4: Choose to suspend or delete the user. Once you're in the user's account details, you'll see options for both suspending and deleting the account.

Suspending a User: To suspend a user, click on the "Suspend User" button. Suspending a user temporarily disables their account, preventing them from accessing Google Workspace services while retaining their data and settings. This option is useful if an employee is on leave or if you need to restrict access temporarily for any reason. To confirm, you'll need to click "Suspend" in the confirmation dialog.

Step 5: Confirm suspension. After clicking the "Suspend User" button, a confirmation dialog will appear. Confirm the suspension by clicking "Suspend" again. The user's account will be disabled immediately, but all their data will remain intact.

Deleting a User: To delete a user, click on the "Delete User" button. Deleting a user permanently removes their account from Google Workspace and deletes all associated data, such as emails, documents, and calendar events. This action is irreversible, so it's crucial to ensure you have backed up any important data before proceeding. In the confirmation dialog, click "Delete" to confirm the action.

Step 6: Confirm deletion. After clicking the "Delete User" button, a confirmation dialog will appear. Confirm the deletion by clicking "Delete" again. The user's account and all associated data will be permanently removed from Google Workspace.

Step 7: Notify relevant parties. It's important to inform relevant team members or departments about the suspension or deletion of the user account. This ensures everyone is aware of the change and can take any necessary actions, such as transferring responsibilities or accessing shared files.

Step 8: Manage data and resources. If you have suspended a user, no further action is needed unless you decide to reactivate their account later. For deleted users, make sure to manage any data or resources that were shared with them. Reassign ownership of important files and documents to ensure continuity in your workflows.

Managing User Roles

Managing user roles in Google Workspace is crucial for delegating administrative responsibilities and ensuring that users have the appropriate level of access to tools and data.

Step 1: Access the Google Admin Console. Start by logging into your Google Workspace account with your administrator credentials. Once logged in, click on the grid icon in the upper right corner to open the Google Apps menu and select "Admin" to enter the Admin Console.

Step 2: Navigate to the Users section. On the Admin Console dashboard, locate and click on the "Users" section. This is where you can view and manage all user accounts within your organization.

Step 3: Select the user whose role you want to manage. In the Users section, find the user account you want to modify. You can scroll through the list or use the search bar to locate the specific user quickly. Click on the user's name to open their account details.

Step 4: Assign or change the user's role. Once you're in the user's account details, you'll see an option to manage roles. Click on the "Roles and Privileges" section. Here, you can assign or change the user's role. Google Workspace offers several predefined roles, such as Super Admin, Group Admin, User Management Admin, and others, each with different levels of permissions.

Step 5: Select the appropriate role. Review the available roles and their descriptions to determine the appropriate role for the user. For example:

- **Super Admin**: Has full access to all administrative features and settings.

- **Group Admin**: Can manage groups and their members.
- **User Management Admin**: Can create and manage user accounts but does not have access to billing or other sensitive settings.

Choose the role that best fits the user's responsibilities and click to assign it.

Step 6: Save changes. After assigning the new role, review your changes to ensure everything is correct. Click the "Save" button to apply the new role to the user's account. The user will now have the permissions associated with their new role.

Step 7: Notify the user. It's a good practice to inform the user about their new role and the responsibilities that come with it. Provide them with any necessary resources or training to help them understand their new administrative functions.

Step 8: Regularly review roles and permissions. To maintain security and efficiency, regularly review user roles and permissions. Ensure that users still require the access levels they have and adjust roles as necessary when responsibilities change or when users leave the organization.

Managing Devices

Managing devices in Google Workspace is essential for maintaining security and ensuring that all devices accessing your organization's data are compliant with your policies.

Step 1: Access the Google Admin Console. Begin by logging into your Google Workspace account using your administrator credentials. Once logged in, click on the grid icon in the upper right corner to open the Google Apps menu, then select "Admin" to enter the Admin Console.

Step 2: Navigate to the Devices section. On the Admin Console dashboard, find and click on the "Devices" section. This area allows you to view and manage all the devices that have access to your Google Workspace account.

Step 3: View the list of devices. In the Devices section, you will see a list of all devices connected to your Google Workspace. This includes mobile devices, laptops, desktops, and any other hardware accessing your organization's data. You can filter this list by device type, status, or user.

Step 4: Inspect device details. Click on any device in the list to view detailed information about it. This includes the device type, operating system, last sync time, and user information. Reviewing these details helps you understand which devices are accessing your data and whether they meet your security standards.

Step 5: Enforce security policies. In the Admin Console, you can set up and enforce various security policies for managed devices. This includes requirements for device encryption, screen locks, strong passwords, and regular updates. Navigate to the "Security" section within "Devices" to configure these settings.

Step 6: Approve or block devices. To maintain control over which devices can access your data, you can manually approve or block devices. In the Devices section, select a device and choose to either approve or block it. Approved devices are allowed to access Google Workspace, while blocked devices are denied access.

Step 7: Wipe data from lost or stolen devices. If a device is lost or stolen, you can remotely wipe its data to protect sensitive information. In the Devices section, select the compromised device and choose the "Wipe Device" option. This action will erase all Google Workspace data from the device, ensuring it cannot be accessed by unauthorized individuals.

Step 8: Monitor device activity. Regularly monitoring device activity is crucial for maintaining security. Use the "Reports" section in the Admin Console to generate reports on device usage, sync status, and compliance with security policies. These reports can help you identify any unusual activity or potential security threats.

Step 9: Manage device settings. In addition to security policies, you can manage various device settings to optimize performance and compliance. This includes configuring Wi-Fi settings, installing required applications, and setting up VPN access. Navigate to the appropriate subsections within "Devices" to adjust these settings.

Step 10: Educate users about device security. Ensuring that users understand the importance of device security is key to maintaining a secure environment. Provide training and resources on best practices for securing devices, recognizing phishing attempts, and reporting lost or stolen devices.

How to Manage Apps

Managing apps within Google Workspace is crucial for customizing the experience for your organization and ensuring that your team has access to the necessary tools while maintaining security and productivity.

Step 1: Access the Google Admin Console. Begin by logging into your Google Workspace account with your administrator credentials. Once logged in, click on the grid icon in the upper right corner to open the Google Apps menu, then select "Admin" to enter the Admin Console.

Step 2: Navigate to the Apps section. On the Admin Console dashboard, locate and click on the "Apps" section. This area allows you to manage all the applications that are part of your Google Workspace environment, including both Google apps and third-party apps.

Step 3: Manage Google Workspace core services. In the Apps section, click on "Google Workspace." Here, you'll see a list of core services such as Gmail, Google Drive, Google Calendar, and Google Meet. You can manage settings for each service by clicking on it. For example, in Gmail settings, you can configure email routing, spam filters, and user permissions.

Step 4: Enable or disable services. You have the option to enable or disable specific Google Workspace services for your users. For example, if your organization does not use Google Sites, you can disable it to simplify the user interface and reduce distractions. To do this, click on the service you want to manage and toggle the settings accordingly.

Step 5: Manage additional Google services. Apart from core services, Google Workspace includes additional services like YouTube, Google Analytics, and Google Photos. In the "Additional Google Services" section, you can enable or disable these services based on your organization's needs. This helps ensure that users have access only to the tools that are relevant to their work.

Step 6: Configure Marketplace apps. Google Workspace Marketplace offers a variety of third-party apps that can integrate with your Google Workspace environment. To manage these apps, go to the "Marketplace Apps" section in the Apps menu. Here, you can browse available apps, install new ones, and manage settings for installed apps. Ensure you review the permissions and security policies of third-party apps before enabling them.

Step 7: Set app permissions and access levels. For each app, you can configure permissions to control how users interact with the app. In the app's settings, specify which user groups or organizational units have access to the app and what level of access they have (e.g., view-only, edit, or admin rights). This ensures that users have the appropriate level of access based on their roles and responsibilities.

Step 8: Monitor app usage and security. Regularly review app usage and security settings to ensure compliance with your organization's policies. In the Admin Console, you can generate reports on app usage, user activity, and security events. These insights help you identify any potential issues or unauthorized access.

Step 9: Update and maintain apps. Keep all apps up-to-date to ensure they function correctly and securely. In the Marketplace Apps section, check for updates regularly and apply them as needed. This helps protect your organization from security vulnerabilities and ensures users have access to the latest features.

Step 10: Provide user training and support. Educate your users on how to use the apps available in Google Workspace effectively. Provide training sessions, tutorials, and documentation to help them understand the features and best practices. This ensures that your team can make the most of the tools at their disposal.

Security Settings

Managing security settings in Google Workspace is essential to protect your organization's data and ensure that all users operate within a secure environment.

Step 1: Access the Google Admin Console. Begin by logging into your Google Workspace account with your administrator credentials. Once you're logged in, click on the grid icon in the upper right corner to open the Google Apps menu, and select "Admin" to enter the Admin Console.

Step 2: Navigate to the Security section. On the Admin Console dashboard, locate and click on the "Security" section. This area allows you to manage all security-related settings for your Google Workspace environment.

Step 3: Configure user security settings. In the Security section, you can manage various user security settings to ensure that all accounts are protected. This includes setting up two-factor authentication (2FA), enforcing strong password policies, and configuring account recovery options. Enabling 2FA adds an extra layer of security by requiring users to provide a second form of verification when signing in.

Step 4: Set up password policies. Password policies are crucial for preventing unauthorized access to accounts. In the Security section, navigate to "Password Management" and configure the policies to require strong passwords. You can set rules for password complexity, minimum length, and expiration periods. Encouraging users to use unique and complex passwords helps protect their accounts from being compromised.

Step 5: Manage device security. Ensuring that all devices accessing your Google Workspace are secure is vital. In the Security section, go to "Device Management" and set policies for device encryption, screen locks, and regular updates. You can also require that all mobile devices accessing Google Workspace use device-level security features like PINs or biometric locks.

Step 6: Configure app security settings. In the Security section, navigate to "App Access Control" to manage which third-party apps can access your Google Workspace data. Review the list of connected apps and restrict access to only those apps that are necessary for your organization's operations. This helps minimize the risk of data breaches through unauthorized applications.

Step 7: Set up data loss prevention (DLP) policies. DLP policies help protect sensitive information from being shared or exposed inadvertently. In the Security section, find the "Data Protection" settings and create rules to monitor and control the sharing of confidential data, such as credit card numbers, social security numbers, or proprietary business information. These rules can trigger alerts or block sharing attempts when sensitive data is detected.

Step 8: Monitor security reports and alerts. Regularly monitoring security reports and alerts is crucial for maintaining a secure environment. In the Security section, access the "Reports" and "Alert Center" to view detailed information on security events, such as login attempts, data breaches, and policy violations. These insights help you identify potential threats and take corrective actions promptly.

Step 9: Manage user roles and permissions. Ensuring that users have the appropriate access levels is key to maintaining security. In the Security section, navigate to "Role Management" and assign roles that limit access based on job responsibilities. For example, only assign administrative roles to trusted individuals who require full access to manage Google Workspace settings.

Step 10: Educate users on security best practices. Educating your team about security best practices is essential for preventing security incidents. Provide training sessions, resources, and guidelines on topics such as recognizing phishing attempts, using secure passwords, and protecting personal devices. Ensuring that users are aware of security risks and how to mitigate them helps create a more secure environment.

Transitioning from Other Services

Transitioning from other services to Google Workspace can seem daunting, but with careful planning and execution, the process can be smooth and efficient.

Step 1: Assess your current setup. Begin by evaluating your current email, calendar, and file storage services. Identify the data and user accounts that need to be migrated. This assessment will help you understand the scope of the migration and plan accordingly. Make a list of all the services you are currently using and note any specific data or features you need to transfer to Google Workspace.

Step 2: Prepare your Google Workspace account. Before starting the migration, ensure your Google Workspace account is fully set up. This includes creating user accounts for all employees, configuring necessary settings, and setting up your domain. Ensure that your Google Workspace environment is ready to receive the migrated data.

Step 3: Choose a migration method. Google offers several tools and methods for migrating data from other services. The method you choose will depend on the type of data and the source service. Common migration tools include:

- **Google Workspace Migration for Microsoft Exchange (GWMME)** for migrating from Microsoft Exchange or Office 365.
- **Google Workspace Migration for Lotus Notes (GWMME)** for migrating from IBM Lotus Notes.
- **Google Workspace Migration for Outlook (GWMO)** for migrating PST files.
- **Google Data Migration Service (DMS)** for migrating email, calendar, and contacts from various sources.

Step 4: Backup your data. Before initiating the migration, it's crucial to back up all your data from the existing services. This ensures that you have a copy of all important information in case anything goes wrong during the migration process. Make sure to back up emails, calendars, contacts, and files.

Step 5: Migrate email data. Using the appropriate migration tool, start by migrating your email data to Google Workspace. For example, if you're migrating from Microsoft Exchange, use GWMME to transfer emails, folders, and attachments. Follow the tool's instructions carefully and monitor the migration process to ensure all data is transferred successfully.

Step 6: Migrate calendar data. After migrating emails, move on to calendar data. Tools like GWMME and DMS can help transfer calendar events, meetings, and reminders to Google Calendar. Ensure that recurring events and shared calendars are also migrated correctly. Verify the accuracy of the migrated data by comparing it with the original calendar entries.

Step 7: Migrate contacts. Next, migrate your contacts using the same tools. Ensure that all contact details, including names, email addresses, phone numbers, and any custom fields, are transferred accurately. Check for any discrepancies and resolve them promptly.

Step 8: Migrate files and documents. For file storage and documents, use Google Drive and Google Drive for Desktop to upload and sync files from your existing storage solutions. If you're using services like Dropbox or OneDrive, you can manually upload files to Google Drive or use third-party tools to automate the process. Organize the files in Google Drive according to your organizational structure to ensure easy access.

Step 9: Test and verify the migration. Once all data is migrated, thoroughly test and verify the migration. Ensure that all emails, calendar events, contacts, and files have been transferred correctly and are accessible in Google Workspace. Address any issues or missing data immediately to avoid disruptions.

Step 10: Train your users. Transitioning to a new platform can be challenging for users. Provide training sessions, resources, and support to help your team get familiar with Google Workspace. Cover essential topics such as using Gmail, Google Calendar, Google Drive, and collaboration tools like Google Docs and Google Meet. Make sure users know how to access their data and perform their daily tasks using the new tools.

Step 11: Decommission old services. Once you're confident that all data has been successfully migrated and users are comfortable with Google Workspace, you can begin decommissioning the old services. Ensure that all critical data has been backed up and that no important information is left behind. Communicate the decommissioning plan to your users and provide a timeline for shutting down the old services.

Step 12: Monitor and support. After the migration, continuously monitor the performance of Google Workspace and address any issues that arise. Provide ongoing support to your users to ensure a smooth transition and help them take full advantage of the new features and capabilities offered by Google Workspace.

Workspace Migration Tool

Migrating to Google Workspace can be a smooth and efficient process when you utilize the Google Workspace Migration Tool. This tool is designed to help you transfer your data from various sources to Google Workspace seamlessly.

Step 1: Prepare for migration. Before starting the migration process, make sure your Google Workspace account is fully set up. This includes creating user accounts for all employees and configuring necessary settings. Ensure that all users are informed about the upcoming migration and have backed up their important data.

Step 2: Choose the appropriate migration tool. Google offers several migration tools tailored to different source services:

- **Google Workspace Migration for Microsoft Exchange (GWMME)** for migrating from Microsoft Exchange or Office 365.
- **Google Workspace Migration for IBM Notes (GWMN)** for migrating from IBM Lotus Notes.
- **Google Workspace Migration for Microsoft Outlook (GWMO)** for migrating PST files.
- **Google Data Migration Service (DMS)** for migrating email, calendar, and contacts from various sources.

Select the tool that best fits your current setup.

Step 3: Set up the migration tool. Download and install the migration tool appropriate for your source service. For example, if you are migrating from Microsoft Exchange, download GWMME from the Google Workspace website. Follow the installation instructions provided by Google.

Step 4: Configure the migration settings. Open the migration tool and sign in with your Google Workspace administrator credentials. You'll be prompted to enter information about your source service. This may include server addresses, admin credentials, and any specific settings required for your current email system. Make sure to follow the instructions carefully to configure these settings accurately.

Step 5: Select the data to migrate. The migration tool will offer options to select the types of data you want to migrate, such as emails, contacts, and calendar events. You can choose to migrate all data or specify a date range to limit the migration to recent data. This flexibility allows you to tailor the migration process to your organization's needs.

Step 6: Map user accounts. The migration tool will require you to map user accounts from your source service to Google Workspace. This involves matching email addresses and user names to ensure that data is transferred to the correct accounts. You can do this manually or use a CSV file for bulk mapping if you have a large number of users.

Step 7: Start the migration. Once all settings are configured and user accounts are mapped, you can start the migration process. Click on the "Start Migration" button to begin. The tool will begin transferring data from your source service to Google Workspace. This process may take some time, depending on the amount of data being migrated.

Step 8: Monitor the migration progress. The migration tool will provide a progress report, showing the status of the migration for each user account. You can monitor this report to ensure that the migration is proceeding smoothly. If any errors occur, the tool will provide details to help you troubleshoot and resolve the issues.

Step 9: Verify the migrated data. After the migration is complete, verify that all data has been transferred correctly. Check emails, contacts, and calendar events in Google Workspace to ensure they match the data from your source service. It's important to address any discrepancies or missing data immediately.

Step 10: Inform and support users. Once the migration is verified, inform your users that the migration is complete. Provide them with guidance on how to access their data in Google Workspace and any changes they need to be aware of. Offer support to help them get accustomed to the new environment and address any questions or concerns.

Step 11: Finalize the migration. After verifying that everything is working correctly and users are comfortable with the new system, you can finalize the migration. This may involve cleaning up any temporary accounts or settings used during the migration process and ensuring that all data is backed up properly.

Gmail

Gmail is at the heart of Google Workspace, serving as a powerful, intuitive, and reliable email platform for your organization. Whether you're managing daily communications, scheduling meetings, or collaborating on projects, Gmail provides a seamless and efficient way to stay connected. In this guide, we'll explore how to set up and optimize Gmail for your team, ensuring you get the most out of its robust features and capabilities.

Setting Up

Setting up Gmail within Google Workspace is a straightforward process that ensures your team can communicate efficiently and securely.

Step 1: Access the Google Admin Console. Start by logging into your Google Workspace account using your administrator credentials. Click on the grid icon in the upper right corner to open the Google Apps menu, and select "Admin" to enter the Admin Console.

Step 2: Navigate to the Gmail settings. In the Admin Console dashboard, find and click on the "Apps" section, then select "Google Workspace." From the list of core services, click on "Gmail" to access the settings for your email service.

Step 3: Configure basic settings. Within the Gmail settings, you'll see several tabs and options. Begin by configuring the basic settings such as organization-wide email settings, which include defining your default email address format, setting up email signatures, and customizing the display language.

Step 4: Set up email routing. Email routing allows you to control how incoming and outgoing emails are handled within your organization. Navigate to the "Advanced settings" tab and look for the "Routing" section. Here, you can set up rules for email forwarding, domain-level routing, and email archiving. These settings ensure that emails are directed appropriately and that important communications are archived for future reference.

Step 5: Configure spam and phishing protection. Google Workspace offers robust spam and phishing protection features. In the Gmail settings, go to the "Spam, phishing, and malware" section. Enable settings such as "Spam filtering" and "Phishing protection" to safeguard your organization's inboxes from unwanted and potentially harmful emails. You can also customize the settings to adjust the sensitivity and actions taken on suspicious emails.

Step 6: Set up compliance and retention policies. Ensuring compliance with legal and organizational policies is critical. In the Gmail settings, navigate to the "Compliance" section. Here, you can configure email retention policies, set up email holds, and define rules for content compliance. These settings help you manage how long emails are retained and ensure that your organization adheres to relevant regulations.

Step 7: Enable email access controls. Controlling who can access Gmail and from where is vital for security. In the Gmail settings, go to the "Access and authentication" section. Set up two-factor authentication (2FA) for additional security, and configure IP whitelisting to restrict access to your Gmail accounts from trusted locations only.

Step 8: Customize user settings. While organization-wide settings are essential, customizing individual user settings can enhance the user experience. In the Admin Console, navigate to the "Users" section and select a user account. Here, you can personalize settings such as email aliases, forwarding rules, and user-specific signatures.

Step 9: Communicate with your users. After configuring Gmail settings, inform your team about the new email system. Provide them with login credentials, instructions on how to access Gmail, and any necessary training materials. This will help ensure a smooth transition and that users are aware of key features and security practices.

Step 10: Monitor and optimize. After setting up Gmail, it's important to monitor its usage and performance. Regularly check the Admin Console for reports and analytics on email activity, security events, and user engagement. Use these insights to optimize settings, address any issues, and ensure that your email system continues to meet your organization's needs.

Sending an Email

Sending an email in Gmail is an intuitive process that allows you to communicate effectively with your colleagues, clients, and partners.

Step 1: Open Gmail. Start by logging into your Google Workspace account. Once logged in, click on the Gmail icon in the Google Apps menu or go directly to mail.google.com. This will open your Gmail inbox.

Step 2: Click on the Compose button. In the top left corner of the Gmail interface, you will see a red button labeled "Compose." Click on this button to open a new email window.

Step 3: Enter the recipient's email address. In the "To" field at the top of the new email window, enter the email address of the person or people you want to send the email to. You can add multiple recipients by separating their email addresses with commas. If you need to send a copy of the email to additional recipients without making them primary recipients, use the "Cc" (carbon copy) field. For sending a blind copy where recipients cannot see each other's addresses, use the "Bcc" (blind carbon copy) field.

Step 4: Add a subject line. The "Subject" field is located just below the "To" field. Enter a brief, descriptive subject line that summarizes the content of your email. A clear subject line helps the recipient understand the purpose of your email at a glance.

Step 5: Write your email message. Below the subject line is the main body of the email where you will write your message. Click in this area and start typing your email. Be clear and concise in your message. Use paragraphs to organize your thoughts, and make sure to address the recipient appropriately.

Step 6: Format your email. Gmail provides various formatting options to enhance the readability and presentation of your email. You can bold, italicize, or underline text, change font styles and sizes, and add bullet points or numbered lists. These options are available in the toolbar at the bottom of the email composition window.

Step 7: Attach files (if needed). If you need to send files with your email, click on the paperclip icon at the bottom of the email composition window. This will open a file picker where you can select files from your computer to attach to the email. You can also use the Google Drive icon to attach files directly from your Google Drive.

Step 8: Add links, images, and emojis. To add a hyperlink to your email, highlight the text you want to link, click the link icon in the toolbar, and enter the URL. To insert an image, click the image icon and choose an image file from your computer or Google Drive. You can also add emojis by clicking the smiley face icon and selecting from the available options.

Step 9: Review your email. Before sending, take a moment to review your email for any typos or errors. Ensure that the message is clear and that you have included all necessary information and attachments.

Step 10: Send your email. Once you are satisfied with your email, click the blue "Send" button at the bottom of the composition window. Your email will be sent to the recipients immediately.

Step 11: Optional: Schedule your email. If you want to send your email at a later time, click the arrow next to the "Send" button and select "Schedule send." Choose the date and time you want the email to be sent, and Gmail will automatically send it at the specified time.

Tracking Email Status

Tracking the status of your emails can be crucial for effective communication, allowing you to confirm that your messages have been delivered and read. While Gmail doesn't offer built-in read receipts for personal accounts, Google Workspace users have access to read receipts, providing valuable insights into email engagement.

Step 1: Enable read receipts in the Admin Console. To allow your organization to use read receipts, start by logging into the Google Admin Console with your administrator credentials. Once logged in, navigate to the "Apps" section, then select "Google Workspace" and click on "Gmail."

Step 2: Configure email read receipt settings. In the Gmail settings, find the "User settings" section. Here, you can enable or disable read receipts for your domain. Enable the option to "Allow email read receipts to be sent" and configure any additional settings, such as allowing read receipts to be sent to addresses outside your organization. Save your changes.

Step 3: Compose your email. Once read receipts are enabled, you can request a read receipt when composing an email. Open Gmail, click on the "Compose" button to start a new email, and fill in the recipient's email address, subject line, and email body as you normally would.

Step 4: Request a read receipt. Before sending your email, click on the three vertical dots (More options) in the lower right corner of the compose window. Select "Request read receipt" from the dropdown menu. This action will notify the recipient that you are requesting confirmation when they read the email.

Step 5: Send your email. After requesting the read receipt, click the "Send" button to send your email. The recipient will receive your message along with a notification that you have requested a read receipt.

Step 6: Receive read receipts. When the recipient opens your email, they will be prompted to send a read receipt. If they agree, you will receive an email notification confirming that your message has been read. The notification will include details such as the recipient's email address, the time they opened the email, and a copy of your original message for reference.

Step 7: Monitor read receipt status. You can keep track of read receipts by checking your inbox for these notifications. This allows you to confirm that important emails have been received and read by the intended recipients. If you do not receive a read receipt, consider following up with the recipient to ensure they received your message.

The Smart Compose & Smart Reply feature

Gmail's Smart Compose and Smart Reply features leverage artificial intelligence to help you write and respond to emails more efficiently. These tools suggest complete sentences as you type and offer quick, contextually relevant responses to incoming messages.

Step 1: Enable Smart Compose. To start using Smart Compose, you first need to ensure it's enabled in your Gmail settings. Open Gmail and click on the gear icon in the upper right corner, then select "See all settings" from the dropdown menu.

Step 2: Navigate to the General settings tab. In the settings menu, click on the "General" tab. Scroll down until you find the Smart Compose section.

Step 3: Turn on Smart Compose. In the Smart Compose section, make sure the "Writing suggestions on" option is selected. This setting allows Gmail to provide predictive text suggestions as you type your emails. Save your changes by scrolling to the bottom of the page and clicking the "Save Changes" button.

Step 4: Use Smart Compose. Now that Smart Compose is enabled, you can start using it to draft emails. As you type in the email body, Gmail will suggest text to complete your sentences. These suggestions appear in light gray text. To accept a suggestion, press the "Tab" key or the right arrow key on your keyboard. This will insert the suggested text into your email.

Step 5: Enable Smart Reply. To use Smart Reply, ensure it is also enabled in your Gmail settings. In the same General settings tab, scroll down to the Smart Reply section and select "Smart Reply on." Save your changes.

Step 6: Use Smart Reply. When you receive an email, Smart Reply will generate suggested responses based on the content of the message. These suggestions appear at the bottom of the email. Click on one of the suggested replies to use it as your response. You can send the suggested reply as is or edit it before sending.

Step 7: Customize Smart Compose and Smart Reply preferences. If you find that the suggestions provided by Smart Compose and Smart Reply are not to your liking, you can customize these features. In the General settings tab, you can turn these features on or off at any time. Additionally, Gmail learns from your writing style and adapts its suggestions over time, becoming more accurate the more you use it.

Step 8: Monitor and refine usage. As you continue to use Smart Compose and Smart Reply, pay attention to how these features enhance your email productivity. If you notice areas where the suggestions can be improved, remember that Gmail's AI will learn and improve with continued use.

Tabbed Inbox

Gmail's Tabbed Inbox is a powerful feature that helps you organize your emails into different categories, making it easier to manage your inbox and prioritize important messages..

Step 1: Open Gmail settings. Start by logging into your Gmail account. Once you're in your inbox, click on the gear icon in the upper right corner to open the Quick settings menu. From there, click on "See all settings" to access the full settings menu.

Step 2: Navigate to the Inbox tab. In the settings menu, click on the "Inbox" tab. This is where you can customize how your inbox is organized.

Step 3: Enable the Tabbed Inbox. Under the "Inbox type" section, select the "Default" option. This enables the Tabbed Inbox feature, which organizes your emails into different tabs based on their content.

Step 4: Customize your tabs. Gmail provides several default tabs, including Primary, Social, Promotions, Updates, and Forums. You can choose which tabs you want to use by checking or unchecking the boxes next to each tab name. Here's a brief overview of each tab:

- **Primary**: Contains emails from people you interact with the most, as well as any messages that don't fit into the other categories.
- **Social**: Includes notifications from social networks, media-sharing sites, and other social services.
- **Promotions**: Contains marketing emails, deals, and offers from various companies.
- **Updates**: Includes notifications such as confirmations, receipts, bills, and statements.
- **Forums**: Contains messages from online groups, discussion boards, and mailing lists.

Step 5: Save your changes. After selecting the tabs you want to use, scroll down to the bottom of the page and click "Save Changes." Your inbox will now be organized into the tabs you selected.

Step 6: Move emails between tabs. Gmail automatically sorts your emails into the appropriate tabs based on their content. However, you can manually move emails between tabs if needed. To do this, drag and drop the email from one tab to another, or right-click on the email, select "Move to tab," and choose the desired tab. Gmail will learn from these actions and improve its automatic sorting over time.

Step 7: Customize tab behavior. You can further customize how each tab behaves by clicking on the tab name and selecting "Customize." This allows you to choose which types of email notifications appear in each tab and adjust other settings to better fit your preferences.

Step 8: Disable or re-enable tabs. If you decide that you no longer want to use the Tabbed Inbox, you can disable it by returning to the Inbox settings and unchecking all the tabs. Your emails will then appear in a single, unified inbox. You can re-enable the tabs at any time by following the steps above.

Step 9: Utilize tab-specific features. Each tab in the Tabbed Inbox has its own features to help you manage your emails more effectively. For example, you can archive, delete, or mark all emails in a specific tab as read with just a few clicks. These bulk actions can save you time and help you maintain a cleaner inbox.

Nudging

Nudging is a useful feature in Gmail that helps ensure important emails don't get overlooked. It reminds you to follow up on messages you haven't replied to and prompts you to respond to emails that haven't received a response.

Step 1: Open Gmail settings. Start by logging into your Gmail account. Once you're in your inbox, click on the gear icon in the upper right corner to open the Quick settings menu. From there, click on "See all settings" to access the full settings menu.

Step 2: Navigate to the General settings tab. In the settings menu, make sure you are on the "General" tab, which is the first tab on the left.

Step 3: Find the Nudging settings. Scroll down the page until you find the "Nudges" section. This section contains the options to enable nudging for your emails.

Step 4: Enable nudging for follow-ups and responses. You will see two checkboxes under the Nudges section:

- **Suggest emails to reply to**: This option prompts you to reply to emails you might have missed.
- **Suggest emails to follow up on**: This option reminds you to follow up on emails you have sent but haven't received a response to.

Check both boxes to enable these nudging features.

Step 5: Save your changes. After enabling the nudging options, scroll down to the bottom of the page and click the "Save Changes" button. Your settings will be updated, and nudging will be enabled in your Gmail account.

Step 6: Use nudging in your inbox. Once nudging is enabled, Gmail will automatically start analyzing your emails and identifying messages that may require follow-up or a response. These emails will be brought to the top of your inbox with a reminder note, such as "Received 3 days ago. Reply?" or "Sent 5 days ago. Follow up?"

Step 7: Respond to nudged emails. When you see a nudged email, you can respond to it directly from the reminder prompt. Click on the email to open it, then compose and send your reply. If the nudge is for an email you sent, you can follow up with a new message or check the status of your initial email.

Step 8: Dismiss nudges if not needed. If you don't need to follow up or respond to a nudged email, you can dismiss the nudge by clicking the "X" next to the reminder note. This will remove the nudge from your inbox without affecting the original email.

Withdrawing an Already Sent Email

Gmail offers a valuable feature called "Undo Send" that allows you to retract an email shortly after you've sent it. This can be a lifesaver if you notice an error or if you've sent the email to the wrong recipient.

Step 1: Open Gmail settings. Start by logging into your Gmail account. Once you're in your inbox, click on the gear icon in the upper right corner to open the Quick settings menu. From there, click on "See all settings" to access the full settings menu.

Step 2: Navigate to the General settings tab. In the settings menu, make sure you are on the "General" tab, which is the first tab on the left.

Step 3: Enable Undo Send. In the General settings tab, look for the "Undo Send" section. Here, you will see an option to adjust the cancellation period. The cancellation period is the amount of time you have to retract an email after you've sent it. You can choose from 5, 10, 20, or 30 seconds. Select your preferred cancellation period by clicking on the dropdown menu and choosing the appropriate time frame.

Step 4: Save your changes. After selecting the cancellation period, scroll down to the bottom of the page and click the "Save Changes" button. This will update your settings and enable the Undo Send feature.

Step 5: Send an email. Compose and send an email as you normally would. After you click the "Send" button, a notification bar will appear at the bottom left corner of your screen, confirming that your message has been sent.

Step 6: Retract the email. While the notification bar is still visible, you will see an "Undo" link next to the confirmation message. Click on the "Undo" link within the cancellation period you selected (5, 10, 20, or 30 seconds). This will retract the email, bringing it back to the draft stage where you can edit it or delete it if necessary.

Step 7: Verify the retraction. Once you click "Undo," a message will appear confirming that the email has been unsent. You can now make any necessary changes to your email and resend it, or discard it if you no longer need to send it.

Using Scheduled Send

Scheduled Send is a convenient feature in Gmail that allows you to compose an email and schedule it to be sent at a later date and time. This is especially useful for managing communications across different time zones or planning emails in advance.

Step 1: Compose your email. Start by logging into your Gmail account and clicking on the "Compose" button to open a new email window. Enter the recipient's email address, a subject line, and the body of your email.

Step 2: Access the Scheduled Send option. Once you have composed your email, do not click the standard "Send" button. Instead, locate the small arrow next to the "Send" button, which will open a dropdown menu.

Step 3: Select Schedule send. Click on the arrow next to the "Send" button to open the dropdown menu, and then select "Schedule send." This will open a scheduling window where you can choose the date and time you want your email to be sent.

Step 4: Choose a date and time. In the scheduling window, Gmail provides a few preset options such as "Tomorrow morning," "Tomorrow afternoon," and "Monday morning." If these options don't fit your needs, you can select "Pick date & time" to set a custom date and time for your email. Use the calendar to choose the date and the time selector to pick the exact time you want your email to be sent.

Step 5: Confirm the schedule. After selecting your desired date and time, click on the "Schedule send" button to confirm. Your email will now be scheduled to be sent at the specified time.

Step 6: Manage scheduled emails. If you need to review or change your scheduled emails, you can do so by navigating to the "Scheduled" folder in your Gmail sidebar. Here, you will see a list of all emails that you have scheduled. Click on any email to open it and make changes if necessary.

Step 7: Edit or cancel a scheduled email. To edit a scheduled email, open it from the "Scheduled" folder, make your changes, and then click the arrow next to the "Send" button to reschedule it. To cancel a scheduled email, open the email and click "Cancel send" at the top of the window. The email will be moved back to your drafts, where you can delete or send it immediately if needed.

Step 8: Verify the scheduled email. After scheduling your email, Gmail will display a confirmation message indicating the time your email is scheduled to be sent. This helps you ensure that the scheduling process was successful.

Priority Inbox

Gmail's Priority Inbox is designed to help you manage your emails more effectively by automatically categorizing your messages based on their importance. This feature ensures that you focus on the most important emails first, reducing clutter and improving your productivity.

Step 1: Open Gmail settings. Start by logging into your Gmail account. Once you're in your inbox, click on the gear icon in the upper right corner to open the Quick settings menu. From there, click on "See all settings" to access the full settings menu.

Step 2: Navigate to the Inbox settings tab. In the settings menu, click on the "Inbox" tab. This is where you can customize how your inbox is organized and choose the type of inbox that best suits your needs.

Step 3: Select Priority Inbox. Under the "Inbox type" section, select "Priority Inbox" from the available options. This will enable the Priority Inbox feature, which sorts your emails into different sections based on their importance.

Step 4: Customize your Priority Inbox sections. Gmail's Priority Inbox divides your emails into several sections by default:

- **Important and unread**: Emails that Gmail identifies as important and that you haven't read yet.
- **Starred**: Emails you have marked with a star to highlight their importance.
- **Everything else**: All other emails that don't fall into the above categories.

You can customize these sections by clicking on the "Options" link next to each section in the Inbox settings. For example, you can choose to show more or fewer items in each section or add additional sections based on your preferences.

Step 5: Set importance markers. Gmail uses various signals to determine the importance of an email, such as who sent the email, how often you email with the sender, and keywords that are often associated with important messages. You can help Gmail learn what's important to you by marking emails as important (using the yellow arrow) or not important (using the gray arrow). This feedback helps Gmail improve its accuracy over time.

Step 6: Save your changes. After customizing your Priority Inbox settings, scroll down to the bottom of the page and click the "Save Changes" button. Your inbox will now be organized according to your new settings.

Step 7: Use Priority Inbox. With Priority Inbox enabled, your Gmail interface will now display your emails in the customized sections. Important and unread emails will appear at the top, followed by starred emails and then everything else. This setup helps you focus on the most critical messages first.

Step 8: Manage your inbox effectively. Regularly review your Priority Inbox and use the importance markers to help Gmail learn your preferences. You can also use other Gmail features, such as labels and filters, to further organize and manage your emails.

Step 9: Adjust settings as needed. If you find that the default sections or settings aren't working for you, return to the Inbox settings tab and make adjustments. You can add or remove sections, change the number of emails displayed in each section, or even switch to a different inbox type if your needs change.

Understanding Labeling

Labeling in Gmail is a powerful feature that helps you organize and manage your emails efficiently. Unlike traditional folders, labels allow you to categorize emails in multiple ways without duplicating them.

Step 1: Access Gmail. Start by logging into your Gmail account. Once you're in your inbox, you can begin creating and managing labels.

Step 2: Create a new label. On the left-hand side of your Gmail interface, scroll down until you see the "More" option. Click on "More" to expand the menu. Then, scroll down and click on "Create new label."

Step 3: Name your label. A pop-up window will appear asking you to name your new label. Enter a descriptive name that will help you identify the category of emails this label will encompass. For example, you might name a label "Project A" or "Invoices." After naming your label, click the "Create" button.

Step 4: Nest labels (optional). If you want to create a nested label (a sub-label under an existing label), you can do so by checking the "Nest label under" box in the pop-up window. Select the parent label from the dropdown menu. Nested labels help further organize your emails into more specific categories.

Step 5: Apply labels to emails. To label an email, go to your inbox and select the email(s) you want to categorize. You can select multiple emails by checking the boxes next to them. Click on the "Label" icon (it looks like a tag) at the top of the page. A dropdown menu will appear with all your existing labels. Check the box next to the label(s) you want to apply to the selected email(s), then click "Apply."

Step 6: Manage labels. You can manage your labels by scrolling down the left-hand menu and clicking on "Manage labels." This will take you to the Labels tab in your Gmail settings. Here, you can edit label names, delete labels, and adjust label settings such as whether the label appears in the label list or message list.

Step 7: Color-code labels. To help visually distinguish between different labels, you can assign colors to them. In the left-hand menu, hover over the label you want to color-code, then click on the three vertical dots that appear next to the label name. Select "Label color" from the dropdown menu and choose a color from the palette. You can also create a custom color if needed.

Step 8: Filter emails by labels. You can quickly find emails with a specific label by clicking on the label name in the left-hand menu. This will display all emails that have been categorized under that label. Additionally, you can use the search bar at the top of Gmail and type "label:[label name]" to find all emails associated with that label.

Step 9: Create filters for automatic labeling. To automate the labeling process, you can create filters that automatically apply labels to incoming emails based on specific criteria. Click on the gear icon, select "See all settings," and go to the "Filters and Blocked Addresses" tab. Click on "Create a new filter," set your filter criteria (e.g., emails from a specific sender or containing certain keywords), and then click "Create filter." Check the "Apply the label" box and select the label you want to apply, then click "Create filter."

Step 10: Use labels for enhanced organization. Regularly review and update your labels to ensure they continue to meet your organizational needs. Labels can be used in combination with other Gmail features, such as stars and filters, to create a comprehensive email management system.

How to use the Spam and Phishing Filters

Spam and phishing filters in Gmail are essential tools designed to protect your inbox from unwanted, potentially harmful emails. These filters automatically detect and filter out spam and phishing emails, reducing the risk of cyber threats and keeping your inbox clean.

Step 1: Access the Google Admin Console. Start by logging into your Google Workspace account using your administrator credentials. Click on the grid icon in the upper right corner to open the Google Apps menu, and select "Admin" to enter the Admin Console.

Step 2: Navigate to Gmail settings. In the Admin Console dashboard, go to the "Apps" section, then select "Google Workspace," and click on "Gmail." This will take you to the settings page where you can manage various aspects of Gmail.

Step 3: Access spam and phishing settings. Within the Gmail settings, click on "Spam, phishing, and malware." Here, you'll find the options to configure your spam and phishing filters.

Step 4: Enable default settings. Gmail's default settings provide robust protection against spam and phishing emails. Ensure that the options for "Spam" and "Phishing" are enabled. This allows Gmail to automatically detect and filter out suspicious emails based on predefined criteria and patterns.

Step 5: Customize spam filter settings. For more control over what gets filtered, you can customize the spam filter settings. In the "Spam" section, you can adjust the sensitivity of the spam filter, choosing to make it more or less aggressive. You can also create custom spam rules to block specific email addresses, domains, or keywords commonly found in spam emails.

Step 6: Configure phishing protection. In the "Phishing" section, ensure that phishing protection is enabled. Gmail uses advanced algorithms to detect emails that may be phishing attempts, such as those trying to steal personal information or trick users into clicking malicious links. You can also enable additional protections, such as identifying emails that spoof your domain.

Step 7: Review and manage quarantined emails. Occasionally, legitimate emails may be mistakenly marked as spam or phishing. In the Admin Console, you can review quarantined emails by navigating to the "Spam and Malware" section. Here, you can release any falsely identified emails to the intended recipients or delete them permanently.

Step 8: Set up custom filters for advanced protection. For more advanced protection, you can create custom filters that automatically label, delete, or quarantine emails that meet certain criteria. To do this, go to the "Filters and Blocked Addresses" tab in Gmail settings, and click on "Create a new filter." Define your criteria, such as specific words, sender addresses, or attachments, and choose the action to be taken on matching emails.

Step 9: Educate users on email safety. Even with robust spam and phishing filters, it's important to educate your users on recognizing and avoiding phishing attempts. Provide training on how to identify suspicious emails, avoid clicking on unknown links, and report phishing attempts to your IT department.

Step 10: Regularly review and update settings. Spam and phishing tactics evolve over time, so it's important to regularly review and update your filter settings. Stay informed about the latest threats and adjust your filters and security policies accordingly to maintain optimal protection.

Google Contacts

Google Contacts is an essential tool within Google Workspace that helps you manage and organize your contacts efficiently.

Step 1: Open your Google Workspace account. Start by logging into your Google Workspace account using your credentials.

Step 2: Access Google Contacts. Once you are logged in, there are a few ways to access Google Contacts:

- **Direct URL**: Go to contacts.google.com directly in your browser.
- **Google Apps Menu**: Click on the grid icon (Google Apps menu) in the upper right corner of your Gmail or Google Workspace homepage. In the dropdown menu, click on the "Contacts" icon. This will open Google Contacts in a new tab.

Step 3: Explore the Google Contacts interface. Once you are in Google Contacts, you will see an interface divided into several sections:

- **Contacts**: This is the main section where you will see a list of all your contacts.
- **Frequently Contacted**: Displays contacts you interact with most often.
- **Labels**: Allows you to categorize your contacts into different groups or labels.
- **Directory**: Shows all contacts within your organization if you're using Google Workspace.

Step 4: Manage your contacts. In Google Contacts, you can add new contacts, edit existing ones, and organize them into labels. To add a new contact, click on the "Create contact" button, enter the contact's information, and save. To edit a contact, click on their name and then the pencil icon to make changes.

Step 5: Sync contacts across devices. Google Contacts automatically syncs with your Google account, so any changes you make will be reflected across all your devices where you use Google Workspace. This ensures that you have up-to-date contact information wherever you go.

How to Organize Your Contacts

Organizing your contacts in Google Contacts helps you manage and find your contacts more efficiently.

Step 1: Access Google Contacts. Start by logging into your Google Workspace account and navigating to Google Contacts. You can do this by going to contacts.google.com or by selecting "Contacts" from the Google Apps menu.

Step 2: Create labels. Labels are like folders that help you categorize your contacts. To create a label, click on "Labels" in the left-hand menu, then click "Create label." Enter a name for your label and click "Save."

Step 3: Add contacts to labels. To add a contact to a label, go to the "Contacts" list, select the contacts you want to organize by checking the boxes next to their names, click on the "Label" icon at the top of the screen, select the label you want to add them to, and click "Apply."

Step 4: Edit contact information. To keep your contacts up to date, click on a contact's name to open their details, then click the pencil icon to edit their information. Update any fields as needed and click "Save" when you're done.

Step 5: Merge duplicate contacts. To clean up duplicates, click on "Merge & fix" in the left-hand menu. Google Contacts will suggest duplicate contacts to merge. Review the suggestions and click "Merge" for each pair you want to combine.

Step 6: Star important contacts. To quickly access important contacts, you can star them. Click on the star icon next to a contact's name to add them to your "Starred" list. You can find all starred contacts by clicking on "Starred" in the left-hand menu.

Step 7: Use search and filters. Utilize the search bar at the top of Google Contacts to find contacts quickly. You can also filter contacts by labels or other criteria to narrow down your search.

How to Add Contacts

Adding contacts in Google Contacts is a straightforward process. Here are the simple steps to do it:

Step 1: Open Google Contacts. Start by logging into your Google Workspace account and navigating to Google Contacts. You can do this by going to contacts.google.com or selecting "Contacts" from the Google Apps menu.

Step 2: Create a new contact. In the Google Contacts interface, click on the "Create contact" button located in the top-left corner.

Step 3: Enter contact information. A form will appear where you can enter the contact's details. Fill in the contact's name, email address, phone number, and any other relevant information. You can also add a photo if you like.

Step 4: Save the contact. Once you have entered all the necessary information, click the "Save" button at the bottom of the form to add the contact to your list.

Step 5: Verify the new contact. After saving, the new contact will appear in your Contacts list. You can search for the contact using the search bar to ensure it has been added correctly.

How to Edit Contacts

Editing contacts in Google Contacts is a quick and simple process. Here's how to do it:

Step 1: Open Google Contacts. Log into your Google Workspace account and go to contacts.google.com or select "Contacts" from the Google Apps menu.

Step 2: Find the contact to edit. Use the search bar at the top to locate the contact you want to edit.

Step 3: Open the contact's details. Click on the contact's name to open their details.

Step 4: Edit the contact information. Click the pencil icon (Edit) in the top right corner.

Step 5: Make the necessary changes. Update the contact's information as needed.

Step 6: Save your changes. Click the "Save" button at the bottom of the form.

3.2.2.3 Deleting Contacts

Deleting contacts in Google Contacts is a simple and quick process. Follow these steps to remove contacts you no longer need:

Step 1: Open Google Contacts. Log into your Google Workspace account and navigate to Google Contacts by going to contacts.google.com or selecting "Contacts" from the Google Apps menu.

Step 2: Locate the contact to delete. Use the search bar at the top to find the contact you want to delete.

Step 3: Select the contact. Click on the contact's name to open their details.

Step 4: Delete the contact. Click on the three vertical dots (More options) in the top right corner of the contact's details page, then select "Delete" from the dropdown menu.

Step 5: Confirm deletion. A confirmation window will appear. Click "Delete" again to confirm and permanently remove the contact from your list.

Alternative method for deleting multiple contacts:

Step 1: Select multiple contacts. In your Contacts list, hover over the contacts you want to delete and click the checkbox next to each one.

Step 2: Delete selected contacts. Click on the trash can icon (Delete) at the top of the screen.

Step 3: Confirm deletion. In the confirmation window, click "Delete" to permanently remove the selected contacts.

Using Labels

Labels in Google Contacts are a powerful tool that allows you to categorize and organize your contacts into different groups.

Step 1: Open Google Contacts. Start by logging into your Google Workspace account. Navigate to Google Contacts by going to contacts.google.com or selecting "Contacts" from the Google Apps menu.

Step 2: Create a new label. On the left-hand side of the Google Contacts interface, scroll down until you see the "Labels" section. Click on the "Create label" button.

Step 3: Name your label. A pop-up window will appear asking you to name your new label. Enter a descriptive name for your label (e.g., "Project Team," "Clients," "Vendors") and click "Save."

Step 4: Add contacts to a label. To add contacts to your new label, go to your Contacts list. Select the contacts you want to organize by checking the boxes next to their names. After selecting the contacts, click on the "Label" icon at the top of the screen.

Step 5: Apply the label. A dropdown menu will appear with all your existing labels. Check the box next to the label you want to apply to the selected contacts and click "Apply." The contacts will now be categorized under the chosen label.

Step 6: View labeled contacts. To view contacts under a specific label, go to the "Labels" section on the left-hand menu and click on the label name. This will display all contacts associated with that label.

Step 7: Edit or delete labels. To edit or delete a label, hover over the label name in the left-hand menu. Click on the three vertical dots (More options) that appear next to the label name. From the dropdown menu, you can select "Rename" to edit the label name or "Delete" to remove the label. Deleting a label does not delete the contacts themselves, only the label categorization.

Step 8: Use labels for email groups. Labels can also be used to create email groups in Gmail. When composing an email, type the label name in the "To" field, and Gmail will automatically add all contacts associated with that label to the email. This is useful for sending group emails quickly and efficiently.

Step 9: Manage label settings. You can manage label settings by clicking on "Manage labels" at the bottom of the Labels section in the left-hand menu. Here, you can create new labels, rename existing ones, and delete labels.

Step 10: Sync labels across devices. Google Contacts automatically syncs with your Google account, ensuring that labels and contact organization are consistent across all your devices where you use Google Workspace.

Merging Contacts

Merging contacts in Google Contacts helps you eliminate duplicate entries and consolidate information into a single contact.

Step 1: Open Google Contacts. Start by logging into your Google Workspace account and navigating to Google Contacts by going to contacts.google.com or selecting "Contacts" from the Google Apps menu.

Step 2: Find duplicates. In the Google Contacts interface, click on the "Merge & fix" option located in the left-hand menu. This option allows Google Contacts to search for and identify duplicate contacts.

Step 3: Review duplicate contacts. After clicking "Merge & fix," Google Contacts will display a list of duplicate contacts it has found. Each pair or group of duplicates will be shown with their respective information.

Step 4: Merge individual contacts. For each pair or group of duplicates, you can review the information before merging. Click on the "Merge" button next to the duplicate contacts you want to consolidate. This will combine the information from the duplicate entries into a single contact, ensuring no data is lost.

Step 5: Merge all duplicates (optional). If you trust Google Contacts' suggestions, you can merge all duplicates at once by clicking on the "Merge all" button at the top of the "Merge & fix" section. This will automatically merge all identified duplicates without needing to review each one individually.

Step 6: Confirm the merge. Once you click "Merge" or "Merge all," Google Contacts will process the merges and consolidate the information into single entries. The duplicates will be removed from your contact list.

Step 7: Verify merged contacts. After merging, it's a good practice to verify that the contacts have been correctly merged. You can do this by searching for the merged contacts in your Contacts list and checking their details to ensure all relevant information has been retained.

Step 8: Edit merged contacts if necessary. If any information is incorrect or missing after the merge, you can manually edit the merged contact. Click on the contact's name, then click the pencil icon (Edit) to update their information. Make sure to save any changes.

Restore Contacts

Restoring contacts in Google Contacts is a useful feature that allows you to recover deleted contacts or revert to a previous state of your contact list.

Step 1: Open Google Contacts. Start by logging into your Google Workspace account and navigating to Google Contacts by going to contacts.google.com or selecting "Contacts" from the Google Apps menu.

Step 2: Access the Restore Contacts feature. In the left-hand menu of the Google Contacts interface, scroll down and click on "Trash." This section contains contacts that have been deleted within the last 30 days.

Step 3: Select contacts to restore. In the Trash section, you will see a list of contacts that have been deleted. To restore a specific contact, hover over it and check the box next to the contact's name. To restore multiple contacts, check the boxes next to each contact you want to restore.

Step 4: Restore the selected contacts. After selecting the contacts you want to restore, click on the "Restore" button at the top of the page. This will move the selected contacts back to your main Contacts list.

Alternative method:

Step 1: Open Google Contacts. Start by logging into your Google Workspace account and navigating to Google Contacts by going to contacts.google.com or selecting "Contacts" from the Google Apps menu.

Step 2: Access the Undo changes feature. In the left-hand menu, click on "More," and then select "Undo changes." This feature allows you to revert your entire contact list to a previous state within a specific time frame.

Step 3: Choose the restore time frame. In the Undo changes window, you will see options to revert your contacts to their state as of 10 minutes ago, 1 hour ago, yesterday, 1 week ago, or a custom date and time. Select the desired time frame and click "Confirm."

Step 4: Verify restored contacts. After restoring, go back to your Contacts list to ensure that the contacts have been restored to their previous state. Check for any missing or incorrect information and make any necessary adjustments.

Syncing Contacts with Other Devices

Syncing your Google Contacts with your smartphone and other devices ensures that your contact information is always up-to-date and accessible wherever you go.

Syncing Contacts with an Android Device

Step 1: Open Settings. On your Android device, open the Settings app.

Step 2: Access Accounts. Scroll down and tap on "Accounts" or "Accounts and Backup," depending on your device.

Step 3: Add your Google account. If your Google account is not already added, tap on "Add account," select "Google," and enter your Google Workspace credentials. Follow the prompts to complete the setup.

Step 4: Sync contacts. If your Google account is already added, tap on "Google" and select your account. Ensure that the "Contacts" toggle is turned on to enable syncing. If it's not already on, turn it on by tapping the toggle switch.

Step 5: Confirm sync settings. Go back to the main "Accounts" or "Accounts and Backup" menu, select "Sync account," and make sure that "Sync Contacts" is enabled.

Step 6: Sync now. To manually initiate a sync, tap on the three vertical dots or "More" option in the upper right corner and select "Sync now." Your contacts will now be synced with your Android device.

Syncing Contacts with an iOS Device

Step 1: Open Settings. On your iPhone or iPad, open the Settings app.

Step 2: Access Accounts & Passwords. Scroll down and tap on "Passwords & Accounts" (or "Mail, Contacts, Calendars" on older iOS versions).

Step 3: Add your Google account. If your Google account is not already added, tap on "Add Account," select "Google," and enter your Google Workspace credentials. Follow the prompts to complete the setup.

Step 4: Enable contact syncing. Once your Google account is added, ensure that the "Contacts" toggle is turned on. This will enable syncing of your Google Contacts with your iOS device.

Step 5: Confirm sync settings. Go back to the main "Passwords & Accounts" (or "Mail, Contacts, Calendars") menu, select your Google account, and ensure that "Contacts" is enabled.

Step 6: Sync now. Your contacts should automatically start syncing. If you want to manually initiate a sync, you can open the Contacts app and pull down to refresh.

Syncing Contacts with Other Devices

Step 1: Open the web browser. On any other device, open your preferred web browser.

Step 2: Access Google Contacts. Navigate to contacts.google.com and log in with your Google Workspace credentials.

Step 3: Sync with third-party apps. Depending on the device and app you're using, look for the option to sync with Google Contacts. This might be found in the app's settings under accounts, sync, or integrations.

Connecting Google Contacts with Other Apps

Connecting Google Contacts with other apps can streamline your workflow and enhance productivity by ensuring that your contact information is consistently updated across all your tools.

Connecting Google Contacts with CRM Systems (e.g., Salesforce, HubSpot)

Step 1: Open your CRM system. Log in to your CRM account (e.g., Salesforce, HubSpot).

Step 2: Access settings. Navigate to the settings or integration section of your CRM system. This is usually found in the main menu or under a user profile dropdown.

Step 3: Find the Google Contacts integration. Look for an option to connect or integrate Google Contacts. This might be labeled as "Google Integration," "Contact Sync," or similar.

Step 4: Authorize the connection. Click on the integration option and follow the prompts to authorize access to your Google Contacts. You will be asked to log in to your Google Workspace account and grant the necessary permissions.

Step 5: Configure sync settings. Once connected, configure the sync settings to specify how and when contacts should be synced. You can usually choose to sync contacts automatically or manually and set preferences for which contacts to sync.

Step 6: Save and start syncing. Save your settings and initiate the first sync. Your CRM system will now start syncing with Google Contacts, ensuring that your contact information is consistent across both platforms.

Connecting Google Contacts with Email Marketing Tools (e.g., Mailchimp, Constant Contact)

Step 1: Open your email marketing tool. Log in to your email marketing account (e.g., Mailchimp, Constant Contact).

Step 2: Access integrations. Navigate to the integrations or connected apps section. This can typically be found in the settings menu.

Step 3: Find the Google Contacts integration. Look for an option to connect or integrate Google Contacts. This might be under "Add New Integration" or similar.

Step 4: Authorize access. Click on the integration option and follow the prompts to log in to your Google Workspace account and authorize access to your Google Contacts.

Step 5: Map contact fields. After connecting, you may need to map the fields from Google Contacts to your email marketing tool. Ensure that fields like name, email address, and phone number are correctly matched.

Step 6: Sync contacts. Initiate the sync process. Depending on the tool, you may have options for one-time syncs or ongoing automatic syncing. Choose the option that best fits your needs.

Step 7: Confirm sync completion. Once the sync is complete, check your contact lists in the email marketing tool to ensure that all contacts have been imported correctly.

Connecting Google Contacts with Project Management Tools (e.g., Trello, Asana)

Step 1: Open your project management tool. Log in to your project management account (e.g., Trello, Asana).

Step 2: Access settings or integrations. Navigate to the settings or integrations section.

Step 3: Find the Google Contacts integration. Look for an option to connect or integrate Google Contacts. This might be listed under "App Integrations" or "Connected Apps."

Step 4: Authorize the connection. Click on the integration option and follow the prompts to log in to your Google Workspace account and authorize access to your Google Contacts.

Step 5: Configure settings. Set up how you want to use Google Contacts within the project management tool. This might involve specifying which contact details to display or how to link contacts to projects and tasks.

Step 6: Save settings and verify. Save your integration settings and verify that Google Contacts are now accessible within your project management tool. Check that contacts are displaying correctly and that the integration is functioning as expected.

Google Chat

Creating chat rooms in Google Chat is a straightforward process that enhances team collaboration and communication within Google Workspace.

Step 1: Open Google Chat. Start by logging into your Google Workspace account and navigating to Google Chat. You can access it directly via chat.google.com or through the Google Apps menu.

Step 2: Start a new room. In the left-hand menu of Google Chat, click on the "+" (plus) icon next to "Rooms." This will open a menu with options to create a new room or join an existing one.

Step 3: Select "Create room." Click on the "Create room" option to start setting up your new chat room.

Step 4: Name your room. A pop-up window will appear asking you to name your room. Enter a descriptive name that reflects the purpose or members of the chat room (e.g., "Project Team," "Marketing Discussions").

Step 5: Add room members. In the same pop-up window, you can add members to the room. Start typing the names or email addresses of the people you want to invite, and select them from the list that appears. You can also skip this step and add members later if you prefer.

Step 6: Set room privacy. Choose the privacy settings for your room. You can make the room discoverable by everyone in your organization or keep it private and invite-only.

Step 7: Create the room. Once you've named your room, added members, and set the privacy settings, click the "Create" button to finalize the setup. Your new chat room will now appear in the Rooms section of Google Chat.

Step 8: Customize room settings (optional). After creating the room, you can customize its settings by clicking on the room name at the top of the chat window and selecting "Room settings." Here, you can manage room members, change the room name, and adjust notification preferences.

Step 9: Start chatting. Begin using your new chat room to communicate and collaborate with your team. You can send messages, share files, and use @mentions to get someone's attention.

Manage Permissions

Managing permissions in Google Workspace is essential for controlling access to data and ensuring that users have the appropriate level of access to perform their tasks.

Step 1: Access the Google Admin Console. Start by logging into your Google Workspace account with your administrator credentials. Click on the grid icon in the upper right corner to open the Google Apps menu, and select "Admin" to enter the Admin Console.

Step 2: Navigate to the Users section. In the Admin Console dashboard, locate and click on the "Users" section. This is where you manage all user accounts within your organization.

Step 3: Select the user. Find the user whose permissions you want to manage. You can scroll through the list of users or use the search bar to quickly locate the specific user. Click on the user's name to open their account details.

Step 4: Access roles and privileges. In the user's account details, click on "Roles and Privileges." This section allows you to assign roles and adjust the user's access levels.

Step 5: Assign a new role. To change the user's role, click on "Assign Roles." You'll see a list of available roles, such as Super Admin, User Management Admin, and Group Admin. Select the appropriate role based on the user's responsibilities and required access level. Click "Save" to apply the new role.

Step 6: Customize privileges. If you need to customize the user's privileges further, click on "Custom Admin Roles" in the Roles and Privileges section. Here, you can create custom roles with specific permissions tailored to the user's needs. Define the permissions and assign the custom role to the user.

Step 7: Manage group memberships. To control access to specific resources or communication channels, you can manage the user's group memberships. In the user's account details, click on "Groups." Add or remove the user from groups as necessary by selecting the appropriate groups and clicking "Save."

Step 8: Set application-specific permissions. For granular control over access to specific Google Workspace applications (e.g., Google Drive, Gmail), navigate to the "Apps" section in the Admin Console. Select the application, and then go to "Settings for Drive and Docs" (or the relevant application). Adjust sharing and access settings based on the user's role and requirements.

Step 9: Review and confirm changes. After making the necessary changes to the user's permissions, review all adjustments to ensure they align with your organization's security policies and access requirements. Confirm that the changes have been applied correctly.

Step 10: Notify the user. Inform the user about any changes to their permissions and provide guidance on how to use their new access levels effectively. Ensure they understand any new responsibilities or restrictions associated with their updated permissions.

Collaboration Features

Google Workspace offers a range of powerful collaboration features designed to enhance teamwork and streamline workflows.

Using Google Docs for Real-Time Collaboration

Step 1: Open Google Docs. Start by logging into your Google Workspace account and navigating to Google Docs. You can access it directly via docs.google.com or through the Google Apps menu.

Step 2: Create or open a document. Click on the "Blank" option to create a new document or open an existing document from your Google Drive.

Step 3: Share the document. In the upper right corner of the document, click on the "Share" button. Enter the email addresses of the people you want to collaborate with. You can adjust their permissions to view, comment, or edit.

Step 4: Collaborate in real-time. Once your collaborators have access, you can all work on the document simultaneously. Each person's cursor will be a different color, and you can see their changes in real-time.

Step 5: Use comments and suggestions. To leave feedback, highlight the text you want to comment on, then click the comment icon or right-click and select "Comment." You can also use "Suggesting" mode to make suggestions that collaborators can accept or reject.

Using Google Sheets for Collaborative Data Management

Step 1: Open Google Sheets. Log into your Google Workspace account and navigate to Google Sheets at sheets.google.com or through the Google Apps menu.

Step 2: Create or open a spreadsheet. Click on "Blank" to create a new spreadsheet or open an existing one from your Google Drive.

Step 3: Share the spreadsheet. Click on the "Share" button in the upper right corner. Enter the email addresses of your collaborators and set their access level to view, comment, or edit.

Step 4: Collaborate in real-time. Collaborators can enter data, create charts, and use formulas simultaneously. Changes are saved automatically, and you can see who is working on which part of the sheet.

Step 5: Use comments and notes. Click on a cell, then click the comment icon or right-click and select "Comment" to add notes or feedback. You can also use the "Insert" menu to add notes to cells.

Using Google Slides for Team Presentations

Step 1: Open Google Slides. Log into your Google Workspace account and navigate to Google Slides at slides.google.com or through the Google Apps menu.

Step 2: Create or open a presentation. Click on "Blank" to start a new presentation or open an existing one from your Google Drive.

Step 3: Share the presentation. Click the "Share" button in the upper right corner. Enter the email addresses of your collaborators and set their permissions to view, comment, or edit.

Step 4: Collaborate in real-time. Collaborators can add slides, edit content, and format the presentation simultaneously. Each person's cursor is a different color, and changes are visible in real-time.

Step 5: Use comments and speaker notes. Click on a slide element, then click the comment icon or right-click and select "Comment" to leave feedback. Use the speaker notes section to add presentation notes that can be used during the presentation.

Using Google Drive for File Sharing and Storage

Step 1: Open Google Drive. Log into your Google Workspace account and navigate to Google Drive at drive.google.com or through the Google Apps menu.

Step 2: Upload or create files. Click on the "New" button to upload files or create new documents, spreadsheets, and presentations.

Step 3: Share files and folders. Right-click on a file or folder and select "Share." Enter the email addresses of your collaborators and set their access level to view, comment, or edit.

Step 4: Manage shared files. Use the "Shared with me" section to view files and folders that others have shared with you. You can also organize shared files into folders for easier access.

Step 5: Collaborate on files. Open a shared file to collaborate in real-time. Use the commenting and suggestion features to provide feedback and make edits collaboratively.

Using Google Meet for Virtual Meetings

Step 1: Open Google Meet. Log into your Google Workspace account and navigate to Google Meet at meet.google.com or through the Google Apps menu.

Step 2: Start a new meeting. Click on "New Meeting" to start a new virtual meeting. You can choose to start an instant meeting, schedule one in Google Calendar, or get a meeting link to share with others.

Step 3: Invite participants. Share the meeting link with participants or add them directly using their email addresses.

Step 4: Collaborate during the meeting. Use the screen sharing feature to present documents, spreadsheets, or slides. Use the chat feature to communicate and share links during the meeting.

Step 5: Record the meeting (optional). If you need to keep a record of the meeting, click the three vertical dots in the lower right corner and select "Record meeting." The recording will be saved to Google Drive.

Formatting Google Chat Messages

Formatting your messages in Google Chat can make your communication clearer and more effective.

Step 1: Open Google Chat. Start by logging into your Google Workspace account and navigating to Google Chat. You can access it directly via chat.google.com or through the Google Apps menu.

Step 2: Select a chat. Choose the individual or group chat where you want to send your formatted message. Click on the chat to open the conversation window.

Step 3: Type your message. Begin typing your message in the text input box at the bottom of the chat window.

Step 4: Apply bold formatting. To make text bold, place an asterisk (*) before and after the text you want to bold. For example, typing *this is bold text* will display as **this is bold text**.

Step 5: Apply italic formatting. To italicize text, place an underscore (_) before and after the text you want to italicize. For example, typing _this is italic text_ will display as *this is italic text*.

Step 6: Apply strikethrough formatting. To apply strikethrough to text, place a tilde (~) before and after the text you want to strikethrough.

Step 7: Create a code block. To format text as a code block, place backticks () before and after the text. For example, typing this is code textwill display asthis is code text`.

54

Step 8: Create a preformatted block. To create a preformatted text block, use triple backticks (``` ` ` ` ```) before and after the text block. This is useful for longer code snippets or preformatted text.

Step 9: Use inline quotes. To add inline quotes, use the greater than symbol (>) before the text you want to quote. For example, typing > this is a quote will display as:

this is a quote

Step 10: Send your message. Once you have formatted your message as desired, press "Enter" to send it.

Step 11: Edit or delete a message (optional). If you need to edit or delete your message, hover over the message you sent, click on the three vertical dots that appear, and select "Edit" or "Delete." Make your changes and save or confirm the deletion.

Sharing Documents in Google Chat

Sharing documents in Google Chat is a simple process that enhances collaboration and productivity within your team.

Step 1: Open Google Chat. Start by logging into your Google Workspace account and navigating to Google Chat. You can access it directly via chat.google.com or through the Google Apps menu.

Step 2: Select a chat. Choose the individual or group chat where you want to share the document. Click on the chat to open the conversation window.

Step 3: Open the attachment options. At the bottom of the chat window, look for the attachment icon, which looks like a paperclip or the Google Drive icon. Click on it to open the attachment options.

Step 4: Choose the document source. You have two options for attaching documents:

- **Upload from your computer**: Click on the paperclip icon, then select "Upload from computer." Browse your files and select the document you want to share.
- **Share from Google Drive**: Click on the Google Drive icon. This will open a window where you can browse your Google Drive files.

Step 5: Select the document. If you're uploading from your computer, browse and select the file. If you're sharing from Google Drive, navigate through your folders, select the document, and click "Insert" or "Select."

Step 6: Set sharing permissions (if using Google Drive). When sharing a document from Google Drive, you may need to set the sharing permissions. Google Chat will prompt you to choose the appropriate permissions:

- **Viewer**: Allows recipients to view the document.
- **Commenter**: Allows recipients to view and comment on the document.
- **Editor**: Allows recipients to view, comment, and edit the document. Select the appropriate permission level and click "Send."

Step 7: Add a message (optional). You can add a message to accompany the document by typing in the text input box before sending.

Step 8: Send the document. Once you have selected the document and set the permissions (if necessary), click the "Send" button (or press "Enter") to share the document in the chat.

Step 9: Verify the shared document. After sending, check the chat to ensure that the document has been shared correctly. Recipients should be able to see the document link or attachment and access it according to the permissions you set.

Step 10: Manage shared documents (optional). If you need to change the sharing permissions after sending the document, go to Google Drive, locate the document, right-click on it, and select "Share." Adjust the permissions as needed and click "Save."

Manage Chat Notification

Managing notifications in Google Chat is essential for staying updated on important messages while minimizing distractions.

Step 1: Open Google Chat. Start by logging into your Google Workspace account and navigating to Google Chat. You can access it directly via chat.google.com or through the Google Apps menu.

Step 2: Access notification settings. In the Google Chat interface, click on the gear icon located in the upper right corner of the chat window. This will open the Settings menu.

Step 3: Navigate to notifications. In the Settings menu, click on "Notifications" to access the notification settings for Google Chat.

Step 4: Choose notification settings for your chats. Google Chat allows you to customize notifications for individual chats and rooms. You have the following options:

- **All messages**: Receive notifications for every message.

- **Only @mentions & direct messages**: Receive notifications only when you are mentioned or receive a direct message.
- **Off**: Turn off notifications for that chat or room.

Select the option that best suits your needs for each chat or room by clicking on the dropdown menu next to each one.

Step 5: Set mobile and email notifications. In the Notifications settings, you can also customize how you receive notifications on your mobile device and via email. Toggle the switches to enable or disable mobile notifications and choose whether you want email notifications for missed messages.

Step 6: Manage notification sounds. If you want to change the sound of your notifications or turn off notification sounds, you can do so in the Notifications settings. Look for the option to manage sounds and adjust it according to your preferences.

Step 7: Customize do not disturb settings. Google Chat offers a "Do Not Disturb" mode to help you focus during specific times. In the Notifications settings, find the "Do Not Disturb" section. Set your preferred times or durations when you do not want to receive notifications. During these times, notifications will be silenced.

Step 8: Use quick settings for individual chats and rooms. You can quickly adjust notification settings for specific chats and rooms without going into the main Settings menu. In any chat or room, click on the three vertical dots (More options) in the upper right corner, select "Notifications," and choose your preferred setting.

Step 9: Save your changes. After customizing your notification settings, make sure to save any changes if prompted. Your new settings will take effect immediately.

Step 10: Review and adjust as needed. Regularly review your notification settings to ensure they continue to meet your needs. Adjust them as necessary based on your current workload and communication preferences.

Adding Bots to Google Chat Rooms

Adding bots to Google Chat rooms can enhance productivity by automating tasks and providing useful information.

Step 1: Open Google Chat. Start by logging into your Google Workspace account and navigating to Google Chat. You can access it directly via chat.google.com or through the Google Apps menu.

Step 2: Select a chat room. Choose the chat room where you want to add a bot. Click on the room name to open the conversation window.

Step 3: Open the room details. In the upper right corner of the chat room window, click on the room name or the arrow next to it to open the room details.

Step 4: Access the bot directory. In the room details panel, click on the "Add people & bots" option. This will open a search bar where you can find and add bots.

Step 5: Search for a bot. In the search bar, type the name of the bot you want to add. Google Chat offers a variety of bots, such as Google Drive, Asana, Trello, and many more. As you type, a list of matching bots will appear.

Step 6: Select the bot. Click on the bot you want to add from the search results. This will add the bot to the chat room and prompt you to confirm the action.

Step 7: Confirm the addition. After selecting the bot, a confirmation dialog will appear. Click "Add" to confirm that you want to add the bot to the chat room. The bot will now appear in the chat room and start responding to commands or performing tasks.

Step 8: Configure the bot (if necessary). Some bots may require additional configuration to work correctly. Follow any prompts or instructions provided by the bot to set it up. This might involve linking the bot to other services or specifying preferences.

Step 9: Use the bot. Once the bot is added and configured, you can start using it. Type commands or keywords in the chat room to interact with the bot. Each bot has its own set of commands and functionalities, which can usually be found in the bot's documentation or help section.

Step 10: Manage bot settings. If you need to adjust the bot's settings or permissions, you can do so by accessing the room details and clicking on the bot's name. This will provide options to customize how the bot operates within the chat room.

Step 11: Remove the bot (if necessary). If you no longer need the bot in the chat room, you can remove it by opening the room details, clicking on the bot's name, and selecting "Remove."

Using Google Chat in Gmail

Using Google Chat within Gmail allows you to streamline your communications by integrating chat functionality directly into your email interface.

Step 1: Open Gmail. Start by logging into your Google Workspace account and navigating to Gmail at mail.google.com.

Step 2: Access the chat settings. In the Gmail interface, click on the gear icon in the upper right corner to open the Quick settings menu. From there, click on "See all settings" to access the full settings menu.

Step 3: Enable Google Chat. In the Settings menu, go to the "Chat and Meet" tab. Under the "Chat" section, select "Google Chat" to enable it. Click "Save Changes" at the bottom of the page. Gmail will refresh, and the Chat interface will appear on the left-hand side of the screen.

Step 4: Start a new chat. In the Chat section on the left-hand side, click on the "+" icon next to "Chat" to start a new conversation. Enter the name or email address of the person you want to chat with, and select them from the list that appears.

Step 5: Create a chat room. To create a chat room, click on the "+" icon next to "Rooms" in the Chat section. Enter a name for the room, add members by typing their names or email addresses, and click "Create."

Step 6: Send a message. Click on the name of the person or room you want to chat with. Type your message in the text input box at the bottom of the chat window, and press "Enter" to send.

Step 7: Format your messages. You can format your messages using markdown syntax:

- **Bold**: Surround text with asterisks (*). Example: *bold text*
- **Italic**: Surround text with underscores (_). Example: *italic text*
- **Strikethrough**: Surround text with tildes (~).
- **Code**: Surround text with backticks (). Example: code text`

Step 8: Share files and links. To share a file, click on the paperclip icon in the chat window, select "Upload from computer," and choose the file you want to share. To share a file from Google Drive, click on the Google Drive icon, select the file, and click "Insert." To share a link, simply paste it into the chat window.

Step 9: Manage notifications. To manage your chat notifications, click on the gear icon in the Chat section and select "Notification settings." Here, you can customize your notification preferences for chat messages.

Step 10: Search your chats. Use the search bar at the top of the Gmail interface to find specific messages or conversations in your chats. Type keywords or the names of people you've chatted with to locate the information you need.

Step 11: Customize chat settings. To further customize your chat experience, click on the three vertical dots in the Chat section and select "Settings." Here, you can adjust your chat theme, manage blocked people, and configure other chat-related settings.

Google Chat Spaces

Google Chat Spaces is a feature within Google Workspace that allows teams to collaborate more efficiently by organizing conversations, files, and tasks in dedicated spaces.

Step 1: Open Google Chat. Start by logging into your Google Workspace account and navigating to Google Chat. You can access it directly via chat.google.com or through the Google Apps menu.

Step 2: Create a new space. In the left-hand menu, click on the "+" (plus) icon next to "Spaces." Select "Create space" from the dropdown menu.

Step 3: Name your space. A pop-up window will appear asking you to name your space. Enter a descriptive name that reflects the purpose or members of the space (e.g., "Project Alpha Team," "Marketing Strategy").

Step 4: Add members. In the same pop-up window, add members to the space by typing their names or email addresses. Select the appropriate people from the list that appears. You can add more members later if needed.

Step 5: Customize space settings. Before creating the space, you can customize the settings by clicking on the gear icon. Here, you can choose whether the space is discoverable by everyone in your organization or by invitation only.

Step 6: Create the space. Once you've named your space and added members, click the "Create" button to finalize the setup. Your new space will now appear in the Spaces section of Google Chat.

Step 7: Start collaborating. In the new space, you can start posting messages, sharing files, and organizing tasks. Type your message in the text input box at the bottom of the space and press "Enter" to send it. You can mention specific members by typing "@" followed by their name.

Step 8: Share files and links. To share a file, click on the paperclip icon in the chat window, select "Upload from computer," and choose the file you want to share. To share a file from Google Drive, click on the Google Drive icon, select the file, and click "Insert." To share a link, simply paste it into the chat window.

Step 9: Create and manage tasks. Spaces integrate with Google Tasks, allowing you to create and assign tasks within the space. Click on the tasks icon (a checkmark) in the right-hand panel, then click "Add a task." Enter the task details, assign it to a member, and set a due date if necessary. Click "Add" to save the task.

Step 10: Use threads for organized conversations. Google Chat Spaces supports threaded conversations, which help keep discussions organized. To start a new thread, click on the "New thread" button at the bottom of the space. Type your message and press "Enter." Replies to the thread will be grouped together, making it easier to follow specific topics.

Step 11: Manage space settings. To adjust settings for your space, click on the three vertical dots in the upper right corner of the space window and select "Manage space." Here, you can rename the space, add or remove members, and adjust permissions.

Step 12: Use notifications wisely. To manage notifications for a specific space, click on the bell icon in the upper right corner of the space window. Choose your preferred notification settings: all messages, only @mentions, or none.

Step 13: Archive or delete spaces. If a space is no longer needed, you can archive or delete it. Click on the three vertical dots in the upper right corner of the space window, select "Manage space," and then choose "Archive space" or "Delete space." Archiving keeps the space available for reference, while deleting it removes all content permanently.

Google Voice

Google Voice is a versatile communication tool within Google Workspace that provides voice calling, text messaging, and voicemail services. It integrates seamlessly with other Google services, allowing you to manage all your communications from a single platform.

Setting Up Google Voice

Step 1: Access Google Voice. Start by logging into your Google Workspace account. Navigate to voice.google.com or select "Voice" from the Google Apps menu.

Step 2: Choose a Google Voice number. When you first access Google Voice, you'll be prompted to choose a phone number. Click on "Get a number" and follow the prompts to select a number based on your preferred area code or city.

Step 3: Verify your existing phone number. Google Voice will ask you to verify your existing phone number. Enter your current phone number and click "Send code." You'll receive a verification code via SMS or phone call. Enter the code in the verification box to proceed.

Step 4: Link your phone number. After verification, you'll be prompted to link your existing phone number to your Google Voice account. This allows you to forward calls from your Google Voice number to your existing phone. Follow the prompts to complete this step.

Step 5: Set up voicemail. Google Voice includes a voicemail service that transcribes messages into text and sends them to your email. To set up voicemail, click on the settings gear icon in the upper right corner, select "Voicemail," and follow the instructions to record a greeting and configure your settings.

Using Google Voice for Calls and Texts

Step 1: Make a call. To make a call using Google Voice, open the Google Voice interface and click on the phone icon. Enter the phone number or contact name you want to call, then click the call button. Your call will be placed using your Google Voice number.

Step 2: Send a text message. To send a text message, click on the text message icon (a chat bubble) in the Google Voice interface. Enter the recipient's phone number or contact name, type your message in the text box, and press "Send."

Step 3: Receive calls and texts. Incoming calls and text messages will appear in the Google Voice interface. You'll receive notifications for incoming calls and messages, which you can answer or respond to directly from the platform.

Step 4: Check voicemail. To check your voicemail, click on the voicemail icon (a cassette tape) in the Google Voice interface. You'll see a list of voicemail messages along with their transcriptions. Click on a message to listen to it or read the transcription.

Managing Settings

Step 1: Access settings. Click on the settings gear icon in the upper right corner of the Google Voice interface to access the settings menu.

Step 2: Configure call forwarding. In the settings menu, select "Calls" and configure call forwarding to direct calls from your Google Voice number to your linked phone number. You can add multiple forwarding numbers if needed.

Step 3: Set up call screening. Google Voice includes call screening options to help you manage incoming calls. In the "Calls" settings, enable call screening to require callers to state their name before connecting. This helps you decide whether to answer the call.

Step 4: Customize voicemail settings. Under "Voicemail" settings, you can record a new greeting, configure voicemail notifications, and enable voicemail transcription to receive text versions of your voicemail messages.

Step 5: Manage notifications. In the settings menu, select "Notifications" to configure how you receive notifications for calls, messages, and voicemails. You can choose to receive notifications via email, SMS, or both.

Step 6: Set do not disturb. To temporarily disable call and message notifications, enable the "Do Not Disturb" feature in the settings menu. This will send calls directly to voicemail and mute notifications during the specified period.

Google Voice is a versatile communication tool within Google Workspace that offers a wide range of features to enhance personal and professional communication. Here are the primary use cases and features of Google Voice:

Use Cases

1. Business Communication: Google Voice provides a professional phone number that can be used for business calls, texts, and voicemails. This allows businesses to maintain a consistent and professional communication channel with clients and partners.

2. Remote Work: With Google Voice, remote workers can make and receive calls and texts from any device, ensuring they stay connected with their team and clients regardless of their location.

3. Personal Use: Individuals can use Google Voice to separate personal and work communications. By having a dedicated Google Voice number, users can manage calls and texts more efficiently.

4. Customer Support: Small businesses and startups can use Google Voice to set up a dedicated customer support line. This allows them to handle customer inquiries and issues efficiently without investing in expensive phone systems.

5. Voicemail Management: Google Voice offers advanced voicemail features, including transcriptions and email notifications, making it easier to manage and respond to voicemails.

Features

1. Voicemail Transcription: Google Voice transcribes voicemail messages into text and sends them to your email. This feature allows you to read voicemails instead of listening to them, making it easier to manage and prioritize messages.

2. Call Forwarding: You can link multiple phone numbers to your Google Voice account and set up call forwarding to any of these numbers. This ensures you never miss a call, regardless of which device you're using.

3. Custom Voicemail Greeting: Google Voice allows you to record a custom voicemail greeting, adding a personal touch to your communication. You can also set different greetings for different groups of callers.

4. Do Not Disturb: This feature lets you temporarily disable notifications for calls and texts. When enabled, calls go directly to voicemail, and you won't receive notifications until you turn off Do Not Disturb mode.

5. Call Screening: Call screening helps you manage incoming calls more effectively. When call screening is enabled, Google Voice will ask the caller to state their name before connecting the call. You can then decide whether to accept or reject the call based on the caller's name.

6. Text Messaging: Google Voice supports SMS and MMS messaging, allowing you to send and receive text messages using your Google Voice number. This feature is available on all devices, including smartphones, tablets, and computers.

7. International Calling: Google Voice offers competitive rates for international calls. This feature is particularly useful for businesses and individuals who need to communicate with contacts in other countries.

8. Integration with Google Workspace: Google Voice seamlessly integrates with other Google Workspace apps, such as Google Calendar and Google Contacts. This integration allows for easy scheduling of calls and management of contact information.

9. Voicemail to Email: In addition to transcriptions, Google Voice can send voicemail audio files to your email. This ensures you have a record of all voicemails and can access them from any device with email access.

10. Number Porting: Google Voice allows you to port your existing phone number to your Google Voice account. This is useful if you want to keep your current number while taking advantage of Google Voice features.

11. Web and Mobile Access: Google Voice is accessible via web browsers and mobile apps, providing flexibility and convenience. You can manage your calls, texts, and voicemails from any device with an internet connection.

12. Spam Filtering: Google Voice includes spam filtering capabilities to block unwanted calls and messages. This helps reduce interruptions and keeps your communication channels free from spam.

Google Drive

Google Drive is a powerful cloud storage service within Google Workspace that enables you to store, share, and collaborate on files from anywhere. It integrates seamlessly with other Google Workspace tools, making it an essential part of your workflow.

Desktop App

The Google Drive Desktop App, known as Google Drive for Desktop, allows you to seamlessly sync files between your computer and Google Drive, making it easy to access and manage your files from any device.

Setting Up Google Drive for Desktop

Step 1: Download the Google Drive for Desktop App. Start by downloading the Google Drive for Desktop App from the Google Drive website. Click on "Download Drive for desktop" and follow the prompts to download the installer.

Step 2: Install the app. Once the installer has been downloaded, open it and follow the on-screen instructions to install Google Drive for Desktop on your computer.

Step 3: Sign in with your Google Workspace account. After installation, open Google Drive for Desktop. You'll be prompted to sign in with your Google Workspace account. Enter your email and password, and follow any additional security prompts, such as two-factor authentication.

Step 4: Choose your sync preferences. Google Drive for Desktop offers two main options for syncing files:

- **Stream files**: This option allows you to access all your Google Drive files directly from your computer without using much storage space. Files are streamed on demand.
- **Mirror files**: This option keeps a local copy of your Google Drive files on your computer. This uses more storage but allows you to access files offline. Choose the option that best suits your needs and click "Next."

Step 5: Set up local folders for backup. Google Drive for Desktop allows you to back up specific folders from your computer to Google Drive. Select the folders you want to back up (e.g., Documents, Desktop, Pictures) and click "Save."

Step 6: Complete the setup. Follow the remaining prompts to complete the setup process. Google Drive for Desktop will now start syncing your files based on the preferences you've set.

Using Google Drive for Desktop

Step 1: Access Google Drive files from your computer. Once Google Drive for Desktop is set up, you can access your Google Drive files directly from your computer's file explorer (Windows) or Finder (Mac). Look for "Google Drive" in the sidebar.

Step 2: Sync files between your computer and Google Drive. To sync files, simply drag and drop them into the Google Drive folder on your computer. Files added to this folder will automatically be uploaded to Google Drive and synced across your devices.

Step 3: Manage synced files. Right-click on any file or folder in your Google Drive folder to access options such as:

- **Available offline**: Make files available offline if you chose the stream files option.
- **View on Google Drive**: Open the file or folder in Google Drive on the web.
- **Share with Google Drive**: Share the file or folder directly from your computer.
- **Get link**: Generate a shareable link for the file or folder.

Step 4: Monitor sync status. The Google Drive for Desktop app icon in your system tray (Windows) or menu bar (Mac) will show the sync status. Click on the icon to view the sync progress, access settings, and see notifications about any issues.

Step 5: Adjust sync settings. To change your sync preferences, click on the Google Drive for Desktop icon in the system tray or menu bar, then click on the settings gear icon. Here, you can adjust preferences, such as which folders to sync, backup settings, and whether to stream or mirror files.

Step 6: Pause or resume syncing. If you need to pause syncing temporarily (e.g., to conserve bandwidth), click on the Google Drive for Desktop icon, then click on the settings gear icon and select "Pause syncing." To resume, select "Resume syncing."

Step 7: Uninstall or update the app. To uninstall Google Drive for Desktop, follow your computer's standard uninstallation process through the Control Panel (Windows) or Applications folder (Mac). To update, the app should automatically update itself, but you can check for updates in the settings menu.

Accessing Google Drive

Google Drive is a powerful tool within Google Workspace that allows you to store, share, and collaborate on files seamlessly. Accessing Google Drive is straightforward and can be done from various devices and platforms.

Accessing Google Drive on a Web Browser

Step 1: Open your web browser. Google Drive is accessible from any modern web browser such as Google Chrome, Mozilla Firefox, Safari, or Microsoft Edge.

Step 2: Go to the Google Drive website. In the address bar of your web browser, type drive.google.com and press Enter. This will take you to the Google Drive homepage.

Step 3: Sign in to your Google Workspace account. If you are not already signed in, you will be prompted to enter your Google Workspace email address and password. Enter your credentials and click "Next." If you have two-factor authentication enabled, follow the prompts to complete the sign-in process.

Step 4: Explore the Google Drive interface. Once signed in, you will see the Google Drive interface, which includes the navigation panel on the left, the main file area, and the toolbar at the top. The navigation panel includes sections such as My Drive, Shared with me, Recent, and Trash.

Accessing Google Drive on Mobile Devices

Step 1: Download the Google Drive app. Open the App Store on your iOS device or the Google Play Store on your Android device. Search for "Google Drive" and download the app developed by Google LLC.

Step 2: Install the app. Once the app is downloaded, install it on your device by following the on-screen instructions.

Step 3: Open the Google Drive app. Locate the Google Drive app icon on your device and tap it to open the app.

Step 4: Sign in to your Google Workspace account. If you are not already signed in, you will be prompted to enter your Google Workspace email address and password. Enter your credentials and follow any additional security prompts.

Step 5: Navigate the Google Drive app. The app interface includes tabs for My Drive, Shared with me, and Recent files. You can tap on these tabs to access different sections of your Google Drive.

Accessing Google Drive for Desktop

Step 1: Download Google Drive for Desktop. Go to the Google Drive website at drive.google.com and click on "Download Drive for desktop." Follow the prompts to download the installer for your operating system (Windows or macOS).

Step 2: Install the app. Open the downloaded installer and follow the on-screen instructions to install Google Drive for Desktop on your computer.

Step 3: Sign in to your Google Workspace account. Once installed, open Google Drive for Desktop and sign in with your Google Workspace email address and password. Follow any additional security prompts.

Step 4: Sync your files. Choose your sync preferences, such as streaming files or mirroring files on your computer. This will determine how your files are synced between your computer and Google Drive.

Step 5: Access files from your computer. Google Drive for Desktop creates a dedicated folder on your computer where you can access your Google Drive files. Open your file explorer (Windows) or Finder (macOS) and look for the Google Drive folder in the sidebar.

How to Use Google Drive

Google Drive is a robust cloud storage solution that allows you to store, share, and collaborate on files seamlessly. It integrates with other Google Workspace apps, making it an essential tool for productivity.

Setting Up

Step 1: Access Google Drive. Start by logging into your Google Workspace account and navigating to Google Drive at drive.google.com or through the Google Apps menu.

Step 2: Understand the interface. Familiarize yourself with the Google Drive interface, which includes the navigation panel on the left, the main file area, and the toolbar at the top. The navigation panel includes sections such as My Drive, Shared with me, Recent, and Trash.

Step 3: Install Google Drive for Desktop (optional). For easier access to your files, you can install Google Drive for Desktop. Download and install it from the Google Drive website, then sign in with your Google Workspace credentials.

Uploading and Managing Files

Step 1: Upload files and folders. Click on the "New" button in the top-left corner of the interface. Select "File upload" or "Folder upload" from the dropdown menu. Choose the files or folders from your computer that you want to upload.

Step 2: Organize files with folders. Create folders to organize your files by clicking on the "New" button and selecting "Folder." Name the folder and click "Create." Drag and drop files into the appropriate folders to keep your Drive organized.

Step 3: Use the search function. To quickly find files, use the search bar at the top of the interface. You can search by file name, type, owner, or keywords within documents. Use the advanced search options by clicking on the filter icon in the search bar.

Step 4: Manage file details. Right-click on a file or folder to access options such as "Preview," "Open with," "Share," "Get link," "Move to," and "Remove." Use these options to manage your files effectively.

Sharing and Collaborating

Step 1: Share files and folders. Right-click on the file or folder you want to share and select "Share." Enter the email addresses of the people you want to share with, and set their permissions to Viewer, Commenter, or Editor. Click "Send" to share.

Step 2: Get shareable links. Right-click on the file or folder and select "Get link." Choose the desired permission level for anyone with the link and click "Copy link."

Step 3: Collaborate in real-time. Google Drive integrates with Google Docs, Sheets, and Slides, allowing multiple people to work on the same document simultaneously. Changes are saved automatically, and you can see who is making edits in real-time.

Step 4: Comment and assign tasks. In Google Docs, Sheets, and Slides, you can highlight text or cells and click on the comment icon to leave feedback or assign tasks to collaborators by typing "+" followed by their email address.

Advanced Features

Step 1: Use version history. Google Drive automatically saves versions of your files. To view or restore a previous version, open the file, click on "File" in the menu, and select "Version history." Choose "See version history" to view and restore earlier versions.

Step 2: Set up offline access. To access files offline, open Google Drive in your browser, click on the settings gear icon, and select "Settings." Enable "Offline" mode. This allows you to access and edit files without an internet connection, and changes will sync when you reconnect.

Step 3: Utilize Google Drive integrations. Google Drive integrates with various third-party apps to extend its functionality. To explore and add integrations, click on the settings gear icon, select "Settings," and go to the "Manage apps" section.

Step 4: Manage storage. Keep track of your storage usage by clicking on the "Storage" option in the navigation panel. Here, you can see how much space you're using and identify large files or unused items to delete and free up space.

Security and Privacy

Step 1: Manage sharing settings. Regularly review the sharing settings for your files and folders. Go to "Shared with me" to see files others have shared with you and adjust permissions if necessary.

Step 2: Use two-factor authentication. Enable two-factor authentication (2FA) for your Google Workspace account to add an extra layer of security. This can be done through the Google Account security settings.

Step 3: Regularly back up important files. While Google Drive offers robust cloud storage, it's good practice to periodically back up critical files to another storage solution, such as an external hard drive or another cloud service.

Uploading Files/Folders to Google Drive

Uploading files and folders to Google Drive is a simple process that ensures your important documents, photos, and other files are stored safely in the cloud. This allows you to access them from any device and share them easily with others.

Uploading Files/Folders from a Web Browser

Step 1: Open Google Drive. Start by logging into your Google Workspace account and navigating to Google Drive at drive.google.com.

Step 2: Select the "New" button. In the top-left corner of the Google Drive interface, click on the "New" button. This will open a dropdown menu with options for uploading files and folders.

Step 3: Choose the upload type.

- To upload individual files, click on "File upload."
- To upload an entire folder, click on "Folder upload."

Step 4: Select files or folders from your computer. A file explorer window will open, allowing you to browse your computer for the files or folders you want to upload. Select the items you wish to upload and click "Open" (or "Upload" on some systems).

Step 5: Monitor the upload progress. Google Drive will begin uploading your selected files or folders. You can monitor the progress in the lower-right corner of the screen. Larger files and folders may take longer to upload, depending on your internet speed.

Step 6: Access uploaded files. Once the upload is complete, your files or folders will appear in your Google Drive. You can organize them into folders, share them with others, or access them from any device with internet access.

Uploading Files/Folders from a Mobile Device

Step 1: Open the Google Drive app. If you don't have the app installed, download it from the App Store (iOS) or Google Play Store (Android).

Step 2: Sign in to your Google Workspace account. If you are not already signed in, enter your Google Workspace email and password to access your Drive.

Step 3: Tap the "+" button. In the lower right corner of the app, tap the "+" button to open a menu with options for uploading.

Step 4: Choose the upload type.

- To upload individual files, tap on "Upload."
- To upload an entire folder (available on Android), tap on "Folder upload."

Step 5: Select files or folders from your device. Browse your device's storage to find the files or folders you want to upload. Tap on the items to select them and then tap "Open" or "Upload."

Step 6: Monitor the upload progress. The app will begin uploading your selected files or folders. You can monitor the progress in the notification area of your device.

Step 7: Access uploaded files. Once the upload is complete, your files or folders will appear in your Google Drive. You can organize them into folders, share them with others, or access them from any device with internet access.

Uploading Files/Folders Using Google Drive for Desktop

Step 1: Open Google Drive for Desktop. If you don't have it installed, download and install it from the Google Drive website.

Step 2: Sign in to your Google Workspace account. Open Google Drive for Desktop and sign in with your Google Workspace email and password.

Step 3: Sync your files. Choose your sync preferences:

- **Stream files**: Access all your Google Drive files directly from your computer without using much storage space.
- **Mirror files**: Keep a local copy of your Google Drive files on your computer, which uses more storage but allows you to access files offline.

Step 4: Drag and drop files or folders. Open the Google Drive folder on your computer (found in the file explorer for Windows or Finder for macOS). Drag and drop the files or folders you want to upload into this folder. Google Drive for Desktop will automatically sync these files to your Google Drive.

Step 5: Monitor sync progress. Google Drive for Desktop will display sync status in the system tray (Windows) or menu bar (macOS). Click on the Google Drive icon to see the upload progress.

Step 6: Access uploaded files. Once the sync is complete, your files or folders will be available in your Google Drive. You can organize them, share them with others, or access them from any device with internet access.

Creating Folders

Organizing your files in Google Drive is essential for maintaining a structured and efficient workspace. Creating folders and organizing your files helps you quickly locate and manage your documents, making collaboration easier and more effective.

Creating Folders in Google Drive

Step 1: Open Google Drive. Start by logging into your Google Workspace account and navigating to Google Drive at drive.google.com.

Step 2: Select the "New" button. In the top-left corner of the Google Drive interface, click on the "New" button. This will open a dropdown menu with various options.

Step 3: Choose "Folder." From the dropdown menu, select "Folder." This will prompt a pop-up window where you can name your new folder.

Step 4: Name your folder. Enter a descriptive name for your folder (e.g., "Project Documents," "Financial Reports," "Marketing Materials"). Click "Create" to add the folder to your Google Drive.

Step 5: Locate your new folder. Your newly created folder will appear in the main file area of your Google Drive. You can now start organizing your files into this folder.

Organizing Files in Google Drive

Step 1: Move files into folders. To move files into your new folder, click and drag the file from the main file area into the folder. You can also right-click on a file, select "Move to," and choose the desired folder from the list.

Step 2: Create subfolders. For further organization, you can create subfolders within your main folders. Open the main folder, click the "New" button, and select "Folder." Name your subfolder and click "Create."

Step 3: Rename files and folders. To rename a file or folder, right-click on it and select "Rename." Enter the new name and click "OK" or "Rename" to save the changes.

Step 4: Use color coding. To visually distinguish between different folders, you can assign colors to them. Right-click on a folder, select "Change color," and choose a color from the palette. This can help you quickly identify specific types of folders.

Step 5: Star important files and folders. To mark important files and folders for easy access, right-click on the item and select "Add to Starred." Starred items will appear in the "Starred" section of the navigation panel, allowing you to find them quickly.

Step 6: Use advanced search. If you have many files and folders, you can use the advanced search feature to locate specific items. Click on the search bar at the top, enter keywords, and use filters such as file type, owner, and modification date to narrow down your search.

Step 7: Organize shared files. Files and folders that others share with you appear in the "Shared with me" section. To organize these files, you can add shortcuts to your My Drive. Right-click on the shared file or folder and select "Add shortcut to Drive." Choose the folder where you want to place the shortcut and click "Add shortcut."

Step 8: Regularly clean up your Drive. Periodically review your Google Drive and remove or archive files and folders that are no longer needed. Right-click on an item and select "Remove" to move it to the Trash. To permanently delete items, go to the "Trash" section in the navigation panel, select the items, and click "Delete forever."

By following these steps, you can create a well-organized structure in Google Drive, making it easier to manage your files and collaborate with others. A clean and organized Google Drive enhances productivity and ensures that you can quickly find and access the documents you need.

Sharing Files and Folders

Sharing files and folders in Google Drive is a powerful feature that enables collaboration and ensures that the right people have access to important documents.

Sharing Files and Folders

Step 1: Open Google Drive. Start by logging into your Google Workspace account and navigating to Google Drive at drive.google.com.

Step 2: Select the file or folder to share. Locate the file or folder you want to share. Click on it to select it. You can also select multiple files or folders by holding down the Ctrl key (Cmd key on Mac) while clicking on each item.

Step 3: Open the sharing options. Right-click on the selected file or folder and choose "Share" from the context menu. Alternatively, you can click the "Share" icon that appears at the top right corner of the screen when the file or folder is selected.

Step 4: Add people to share with. In the sharing dialog box, enter the email addresses of the people you want to share the file or folder with. As you type, Google Drive will suggest contacts from your Google Contacts list.

Step 5: Set permissions. Next to each email address you've added, there will be a dropdown menu where you can set the permission level:

- **Viewer**: People can view the file or folder but cannot make any changes.
- **Commenter**: People can view and add comments to the file but cannot make any changes to the content.
- **Editor**: People can make changes to the file or folder, including editing, commenting, and sharing with others.

Choose the appropriate permission level for each person.

Step 6: Add a message (optional). You can include a message with the invitation to provide context or instructions to the recipients. This step is optional but can be helpful for clarity.

Step 7: Send the invitation. Click "Send" to share the file or folder with the specified people. They will receive an email notification with a link to access the shared item.

Generating Shareable Links

Step 1: Select the file or folder. Locate and select the file or folder you want to share in Google Drive.

Step 2: Open the sharing options. Right-click on the selected item and choose "Get link" from the context menu. Alternatively, click the "Get link" icon that appears at the top right corner of the screen when the item is selected.

Step 3: Set link permissions. In the link-sharing dialog box, you'll see a dropdown menu with permission options:

- **Restricted**: Only people you add can open the link.
- **Anyone with the link**: Anyone who has the link can view, comment, or edit, depending on the permission level you set.

Choose "Anyone with the link" if you want to make the link accessible to a broader audience.

Step 4: Adjust permissions. Next to the link-sharing settings, there will be a dropdown menu where you can set the permission level for anyone with the link:

- **Viewer**: People with the link can view the file or folder.
- **Commenter**: People with the link can view and add comments.
- **Editor**: People with the link can make changes.

Choose the appropriate permission level.

Step 5: Copy the link. Click "Copy link" to copy the shareable link to your clipboard. You can then paste this link into an email, chat, or document to share it with others.

Step 6: Share the link. Distribute the copied link to the intended recipients. They can use the link to access the shared file or folder based on the permissions you've set.

Managing Shared Files and Folders

Step 1: View shared files. To see files and folders others have shared with you, click on "Shared with me" in the navigation panel on the left side of Google Drive. This section displays all items that have been shared with your account.

Step 2: Adjust sharing settings. To change the sharing settings of a file or folder, select it, right-click, and choose "Share." In the sharing dialog box, you can add or remove people, change permissions, and generate a new shareable link.

Step 3: Stop sharing. If you no longer want to share a file or folder, you can stop sharing it by removing all collaborators and disabling the shareable link. Open the sharing dialog box, click the "X" next to each collaborator's name, and set the link sharing to "Restricted."

Step 4: Monitor activity. Google Drive provides an activity feed that shows recent changes and actions taken on your files. To view the activity feed, select a file or folder, and click on the "Activity" icon (a small clock) in the upper right corner. This feed helps you keep track of who has accessed or modified your shared items.

Google One

Google One is a subscription service that provides expanded storage, additional features, and enhanced support across Google products. It's particularly beneficial for users who require more storage than what is offered for free with Google Workspace or personal Google accounts.

How to Use Google One

Step 1: To begin using Google One, navigate to the Google One website at one.google.com. Sign in with your Google Workspace or personal Google account. Once logged in, review the available storage plans and select one that meets your needs. Google One offers various tiers of storage, starting from 100 GB to several terabytes. Follow the prompts to subscribe to your chosen plan, providing payment information to complete the subscription.

Step 2: Access Google One via its website at one.google.com or by downloading the Google One app from the App Store (iOS) or Google Play Store (Android). Sign in with your Google account associated with your Google One subscription.

Step 3: On the Google One dashboard, you will see an overview of your total storage usage across Google Drive, Gmail, and Google Photos. Click on "Manage storage" to see detailed information about how your storage is being used. Identify large files, emails, and photos that are taking up space, and use the provided tools to delete unnecessary files and emails. Google One offers suggestions for freeing up space, such as deleting spam emails, large attachments, and duplicate photos.

Step 4: To share your storage plan with family members, go to the "Settings" tab on the Google One dashboard and set up family sharing. Under "Family sharing," click on "Manage family group" and follow the prompts to invite family members to join your Google One plan. You can control what each family member can do, such as managing the shared storage or accessing other Google services.

Step 5: Take advantage of additional features offered by Google One. Google One subscribers have access to Google Experts for help with Google products and services. To contact support, go to the "Support" tab on the Google One dashboard and choose your preferred method of contact (chat, phone, or email). Some Google One plans include access to a VPN for enhanced online privacy. To activate the VPN, open the Google One app, go to the "Benefits" tab, and follow the instructions to set up and use the VPN on your device. Google One subscribers may also receive exclusive offers and discounts on Google products and services. Check the "Benefits" tab regularly to see the latest offers available to you.

Step 6: Use the Google One app to back up your Android or iOS device. Open the app, go to the "Backup" tab, and turn on backup. You can choose to back up your photos, videos, contacts, and calendar events. Manage your backups through the Google One app or website, view the status of your backups, restore data to your device, or delete old backups to free up space.

Step 7: If you need more or less storage, you can easily upgrade or downgrade your Google One plan. Go to the "Settings" tab on the Google One dashboard, click on "Change plan," and select a new storage tier. Follow the prompts to complete the process. You can also update your billing information and view your payment history under the "Settings" tab.

Step 8: Regularly check your Google One dashboard to monitor your storage usage and make sure you're not exceeding your limits. Use Google's optimization tools and suggestions to keep your storage organized and efficient.

Google Photos

Google Photos is a powerful tool within Google Workspace that helps you store, organize, and share your photos and videos. It offers various features to make managing your visual content easy and accessible from any device.

Step 1: To begin, access Google Photos by visiting photos.google.com on your web browser or by downloading the Google Photos app from the App Store (iOS) or Google Play Store (Android). Sign in with your Google Workspace or personal Google account.

Step 2: Once you're signed in, you'll be greeted with the main interface of Google Photos. This includes sections such as Photos, Albums, For you, Sharing, and Library. The Photos section displays all your uploaded images and videos in chronological order.

Step 3: To upload photos and videos, click on the "Upload" button in the top-right corner of the web interface, or tap on the "+" icon in the mobile app. You can select files from your computer, smartphone, or directly from Google Drive. On mobile devices, you can also enable automatic backup and sync to upload new photos and videos automatically.

Step 4: Organize your content by creating albums. Click on the "Albums" tab, then select "Create album." Name your album and add photos and videos by selecting them from your library. Albums help you categorize and find your photos easily.

Step 5: Use the search function to quickly find specific photos or videos. Google Photos uses advanced machine learning to identify objects, places, and even people in your images. Type keywords or phrases into the search bar, and Google Photos will display relevant results.

Step 6: Edit your photos directly within Google Photos. Click on any photo to open it, then click on the edit icon (a pencil) to access editing tools. You can adjust brightness, contrast, color, and more. Additionally, you can apply filters to enhance your photos with a single click.

Step 7: Share your photos and albums with others. Select the photos or albums you want to share, click on the share icon, and enter the email addresses of the recipients. You can also generate a shareable link that can be sent via text, email, or social media.

Step 8: Explore the "For you" tab, which offers automatic creations like collages, animations, and movies made from your photos and videos. Google Photos periodically generates these creations based on your content, providing fun and engaging ways to relive your memories.

Step 9: Manage your storage by regularly reviewing your photos and videos. Google Photos provides tools to help you free up space by identifying large files, duplicate images, and blurry photos. Use these tools to keep your library organized and efficient.

Step 10: Back up your photos and videos. In the settings menu, enable "Back up & sync" to ensure that all your visual content is safely stored in the cloud. This feature automatically saves new photos and videos to Google Photos, protecting them from device loss or damage.

Uploading Photos and Videos

Uploading photos and videos to Google Photos is an essential step to ensure your visual memories are stored safely in the cloud and accessible from any device.

Uploading from a Web Browser

Step 1: Open your web browser and navigate to photos.google.com. Sign in with your Google Workspace or personal Google account.

Step 2: Once you're signed in, you'll be taken to the main Google Photos interface. Look for the "Upload" button in the top-right corner of the screen and click on it.

Step 3: A dropdown menu will appear. Choose "Computer" to upload files from your computer. This will open your file explorer (Windows) or Finder (Mac).

Step 4: Browse your computer and select the photos and videos you want to upload. You can select multiple files by holding down the Ctrl key (Cmd key on Mac) while clicking on each file. Once you've selected the files, click "Open."

Step 5: Google Photos will begin uploading your selected files. You can monitor the upload progress in the bottom-left corner of the screen. Once the upload is complete, the photos and videos will appear in your Google Photos library.

Uploading from a Mobile Device

Step 1: Download the Google Photos app from the App Store (iOS) or Google Play Store (Android) if you haven't already. Open the app and sign in with your Google Workspace or personal Google account.

Step 2: On the main screen of the Google Photos app, tap on your profile picture or initials in the top-right corner to access your account settings.

Step 3: Tap on "Photos settings" or "Settings" and then select "Back up & sync."

Step 4: Toggle the "Back up & sync" switch to the on position. This will enable automatic backup of photos and videos from your device to Google Photos.

Step 5: To manually upload specific photos or videos, go back to the main screen of the app and tap on the "Library" tab at the bottom. Select the photos or videos you want to upload by tapping on them.

Step 6: Tap on the upload icon (a cloud with an upward arrow) located at the top of the screen. Your selected photos and videos will begin uploading to Google Photos. You can monitor the upload progress within the app.

Uploading from Google Drive

Step 1: Open your web browser and navigate to photos.google.com. Sign in with your Google Workspace or personal Google account.

Step 2: Click on the "Upload" button in the top-right corner of the screen and select "Google Drive" from the dropdown menu.

Step 3: A new window will open, showing your Google Drive files. Browse your Google Drive and select the photos and videos you want to upload to Google Photos.

Step 4: Click the "Upload" button. Google Photos will begin importing the selected files from Google Drive. You can monitor the progress in the bottom-left corner of the screen.

Managing Uploaded Photos and Videos

Step 1: After uploading, your photos and videos will appear in your Google Photos library. You can organize them by creating albums. Click on "Albums" in the left-hand menu, then click "Create album." Name your album and add photos and videos by selecting them from your library.

Step 2: Use the search bar at the top to find specific photos or videos. Google Photos uses advanced machine learning to identify objects, places, and people in your images, making it easy to locate specific content.

Step 3: Edit your photos directly within Google Photos. Click on any photo to open it, then click on the edit icon (a pencil) to access editing tools. Adjust brightness, contrast, color, and apply filters as needed.

Step 4: Share your photos and albums with others. Select the photos or albums you want to share, click on the share icon, and enter the email addresses of the recipients. You can also generate a shareable link to send via text, email, or social media.

Organizing Your Photos and Videos

Organizing your photos and videos in Google Photos helps you manage your visual content efficiently and makes it easy to locate specific memories.

Step 1: Open Google Photos. Start by logging into your Google Workspace or personal Google account on photos.google.com or by opening the Google Photos app on your mobile device.

Step 2: Review your library. Once logged in, you'll see all your uploaded photos and videos displayed in chronological order. Take some time to scroll through your library and familiarize yourself with the layout and organization.

Step 3: Create albums. To create an album, click on the "Albums" tab on the left-hand side of the web interface or at the bottom of the mobile app. Click on "Create album," then name your album (e.g., "Family Vacation 2025," "Birthday Party," "Work Projects"). Select the photos and videos you want to include in this album by clicking on them, then click "Done" (web) or tap "Add" (mobile).

Step 4: Add photos to existing albums. To add more photos or videos to an existing album, open the album, click the "Add photos" button (web) or tap the "Add photos" icon (mobile), and select the items you want to add. Click "Done" or tap "Add" when finished.

Step 5: Use face grouping. Google Photos can automatically group photos of the same person together using facial recognition technology. To enable this feature, go to "Settings" by clicking on your profile picture or initials, then select "Group similar faces." Once enabled, Google Photos will group photos of the same person, making it easier to organize and find specific photos.

Step 6: Utilize the search function. The search bar at the top of Google Photos uses advanced machine learning to identify objects, places, and people in your images. Type keywords or phrases such as "beach," "dog," or "John's birthday" to quickly find relevant photos and videos.

Step 7: Label and tag photos. You can manually label and tag photos for easier searching. Click on a photo to open it, then click on the "i" icon (web) or swipe up (mobile) to add a description or tags. This metadata will help you find photos using the search function later.

Step 8: Use Google Photos' "For you" feature. The "For you" tab automatically creates albums, collages, animations, and movies from your photos and videos. These creations are based on themes and patterns identified in your library, providing fun and engaging ways to organize and enjoy your memories.

Step 9: Archive unnecessary photos. To keep your main library organized and clutter-free, consider archiving photos that you don't need to see regularly but don't want to delete. Select the photos you want to archive, click on the three-dot menu, and choose "Archive." Archived photos remain accessible through the "Archive" section.

Step 10: Delete unwanted photos. Regularly review your library and delete any blurry, duplicate, or unwanted photos and videos. Select the items you want to delete, click on the trash can icon, and confirm the deletion. This helps keep your library organized and frees up storage space.

Step 11: Share albums and photos. Organizing isn't just for your own benefit; it also makes sharing easier. Select the photos or albums you want to share, click on the share icon, and enter the email addresses of the recipients. You can also generate a shareable link that can be sent via text, email, or social media.

Step 12: Backup and sync settings. Ensure your photos and videos are always backed up and synchronized across devices. Go to "Settings" and enable "Backup & sync." Choose the upload size (high quality or original quality) and configure other backup settings as needed.

Sharing Photos and Videos

Sharing photos and videos in Google Photos is a straightforward process that allows you to effortlessly share your memories with friends, family, and colleagues.

Step 1: Open Google Photos. Start by logging into your Google Workspace or personal Google account on photos.google.com or by opening the Google Photos app on your mobile device.

Step 2: Select the photos and videos to share. Navigate to your library and select the photos and videos you want to share. On the web, hover over the images and click on the checkmark that appears in the upper left corner of each image. On mobile, tap and hold the images to select them. You can select multiple items at once.

Step 3: Click on the share icon. Once you have selected the photos and videos you want to share, click on the share icon, which looks like a paper airplane on the web or a share button on mobile. This will open the sharing options.

Step 4: Choose the sharing method. Google Photos provides several ways to share your photos and videos:

- **Share via link**: You can generate a shareable link that you can send via email, text, or social media. To do this, click on "Create link" (web) or "Get link" (mobile). Copy the link and share it with your desired recipients.
- **Share directly with Google contacts**: Enter the email addresses of the people you want to share with. Google Photos will suggest contacts from your Google Contacts list. Select the recipients and click "Send" (web) or "Send" (mobile).
- **Add to a shared album**: If you want to share multiple photos and videos over time, consider creating a shared album. Click on "Add to album" and either select an existing shared album or create a new one. Add the photos and videos to the album and share the album link with your desired recipients.

Step 5: Set sharing permissions. When sharing directly with Google contacts or adding to a shared album, you can set permissions to control what recipients can do with your photos and videos. Choose whether recipients can add their own photos and videos to the album, comment on the shared items, or just view them.

Step 6: Share via social media or messaging apps. Google Photos allows you to share directly to various social media platforms and messaging apps. Click on the social media or app icons within the sharing menu to share your selected photos and videos directly to those platforms.

Step 7: Manage shared items. To view and manage the photos and videos you have shared, click on the "Sharing" tab on the left-hand side of the web interface or at the bottom of the mobile app. Here, you can see all the items you've shared and with whom. You can also adjust sharing settings, add or remove collaborators, and stop sharing items.

Step 8: Receive shared items. When others share photos and videos with you, you'll receive a notification in Google Photos. Click on the "Sharing" tab to view shared items. You can add these shared items to your own library by clicking "Save to library."

Step 9: Organize shared items. To keep your shared items organized, create shared albums for different events or groups. Add photos and videos to these albums as needed and invite others to contribute. This is especially useful for collaborative projects or family photo collections.

Step 10: Privacy and security. Be mindful of the privacy settings for shared items. When creating a shareable link, remember that anyone with the link can view the shared items. For more controlled sharing, use direct sharing with specific contacts or shared albums with set permissions.

Managing Storage

Managing storage in Google Photos is crucial to ensure you have enough space for all your photos and videos while keeping your library organized and clutter-free.

Step 1: Open Google Photos. Start by logging into your Google Workspace or personal Google account on photos.google.com or by opening the Google Photos app on your mobile device.

Step 2: Check your storage usage. On the web, click on the settings gear icon in the top-right corner and select "Settings." Under the "Storage" section, you'll see how much storage you've used and how much is available. On mobile, tap your profile picture or initials in the top-right corner, then tap "Photos settings" and "Back up & sync." Here, you'll find your storage details.

Step 3: Review and delete unnecessary photos and videos. Regularly go through your library to identify and delete blurry, duplicate, or unwanted photos and videos. Select the items you want to delete, click on the trash can icon, and confirm the deletion. This helps free up space and keep your library organized.

Step 4: Use the storage management tool. Google Photos offers a built-in storage management tool that helps you identify and delete items that are taking up space. On the web, go to the "Settings" menu and click on "Manage storage." On mobile, go to "Photos settings" and then "Back up & sync." Tap "Manage storage." This tool highlights large files, blurry photos, and screenshots that you can delete to free up space.

Step 5: Optimize your photo and video quality. Under the "Back up & sync" settings, you can choose between "High quality" and "Original quality" for your uploads. "High quality" compresses your photos and videos to save space while maintaining good quality. "Original quality" uploads files in their full resolution but uses more storage. If you're running out of space, consider switching to "High quality."

Step 6: Archive photos and videos. To keep your main library clutter-free without deleting items, you can archive photos and videos. Select the items you want to archive, click on the three-dot menu, and choose "Archive." Archived items are moved to the "Archive" section and are still accessible but not displayed in your main library view.

Step 7: Upgrade your storage plan. If you frequently run out of space, consider upgrading your storage plan. Google One offers various storage plans that provide additional space for Google Photos, Google Drive, and Gmail. Go to one.google.com, sign in with your Google account, and choose a plan that suits your needs. Follow the prompts to subscribe and increase your storage capacity.

Step 8: Regularly back up your photos and videos. Ensure that your important photos and videos are always backed up to Google Photos. Enable "Back up & sync" in the settings to automatically upload new photos and videos to the cloud. This not only protects your files but also helps manage storage on your device.

Step 9: Use Google Photos' cleaning suggestions. Google Photos periodically provides suggestions to clean up your library. These suggestions might include deleting large files, old screenshots, and items with poor quality. Follow these suggestions to optimize your storage.

Step 10: Monitor shared items. Shared photos and videos can also take up space in your Google Photos account. Go to the "Sharing" tab to review shared items. If you no longer need access to certain shared items, remove them from your account to free up space.

Step 11: Manage your Google Drive and Gmail storage. Google Photos shares storage space with Google Drive and Gmail. Regularly check and manage your storage usage in these services to ensure you have enough space. Delete unnecessary files and emails, and consider archiving or backing up important items externally.

Google Vault

Google Vault is an essential tool within Google Workspace designed for data retention, eDiscovery, and compliance. It allows organizations to retain, search, and export data to meet legal and regulatory requirements.

How to Use Google Vault

Step 1: Access Google Vault. Start by logging into your Google Workspace account. Navigate to the Google Vault at vault.google.com. You must have the necessary administrative privileges to access and use Google Vault.

Step 2: Understand the interface. The Google Vault interface includes several key sections such as Matters, Retention, Holds, and Reports. Familiarize yourself with these sections to navigate and use Google Vault efficiently.

Step 3: Create a new matter. Matters are used to organize your Vault activities. To create a new matter, click on the "Matters" tab, then click on the "Create" button. Name your matter and provide a description if necessary. Click "Create" to set up your new matter.

Step 4: Set retention rules. Retention rules specify how long data is retained before it is deleted. To set retention rules, go to the "Retention" tab within your matter. Click "Create retention rule," then specify the conditions for the rule, such as the data type (e.g., Gmail, Drive), the organizational unit, and the retention duration. Choose whether to retain or purge data after the specified period and click "Save" to apply the rule.

Step 5: Apply holds. Holds prevent data from being deleted, regardless of retention rules, until the hold is removed. To apply a hold, go to the "Holds" tab within your matter. Click "Create hold," then specify the data type, the users or organizational units to which the hold applies, and any additional conditions such as date ranges or keywords. Click "Create" to apply the hold.

Step 6: Search for data. To search for specific data, go to the "Search" tab within your matter. Enter your search criteria, including the data type, keywords, date ranges, and specific accounts or organizational units. Use advanced search options to refine your search. Click "Search" to retrieve the results.

Step 7: Review and export search results. Once the search is complete, review the results to ensure they meet your requirements. To export the search results, click on the "Export" button. Choose the export format and click "Create export." Google Vault will prepare the export, and you can download the data once it's ready.

Step 8: Manage and monitor matters. Regularly review your matters to ensure they are up-to-date and compliant with your organization's policies. Go to the "Matters" tab to see a list of all matters. Click on a matter to view its details, including retention rules, holds, and search results.

Step 9: Generate and review reports. Google Vault provides various reports to help you monitor and manage your data. To generate a report, go to the "Reports" tab. Select the type of report you need, such as audit reports or export reports, and specify the report parameters. Click "Generate report" to create the report, then review it to gain insights into your Vault activities.

Step 10: Ensure compliance with legal and regulatory requirements. Use Google Vault to maintain compliance with legal and regulatory requirements by ensuring that all relevant data is retained and accessible. Regularly review and update your retention rules and holds to align with changing requirements.

Step 11: Train and support users. Provide training and support to users within your organization to ensure they understand how to use Google Vault effectively. This includes administrators responsible for setting up and managing Vault, as well as legal and compliance teams who may need to perform searches and exports.

Google Takeout

Google Takeout is a service provided by Google that allows you to export and download your data from various Google services. This tool is particularly useful for creating backups, transferring data to another service, or simply for keeping personal copies of your information.

How to Use Takeout

Step 1: Access Google Takeout. Start by logging into your Google Workspace or personal Google account. Navigate to Google Takeout at takeout.google.com.

Step 2: Select data to include. On the main Google Takeout page, you'll see a list of Google services from which you can export data. By default, all services are selected. To customize your export, click on "Deselect all" at the top of the list. Then, scroll through the list and check the boxes next to the services you want to include in your export. Each service has a dropdown menu where you can specify which data subsets to include, such as specific folders in Google Drive or specific calendars in Google Calendar.

Step 3: Customize your export. After selecting the data to include, scroll to the bottom of the page and click on "Next step." Here, you can customize how your data will be exported. Choose the file type (e.g., .zip or .tgz), the file size (e.g., 2GB, 10GB), and the delivery method (e.g., download link via email, add to Drive, Dropbox, OneDrive, or Box).

Step 4: Create your export. Once you've customized your export settings, click on "Create export." Google Takeout will begin preparing your data. This process may take some time, depending on the amount and complexity of the data being exported. You will receive an email notification when your export is ready.

Step 5: Download your data. When your export is complete, you will receive an email with a link to download your data. Click on the link in the email to go to the Google Takeout page. On this page, you'll see a list of all your exports. Click on the "Download" button next to the export you want to download. If you selected multiple export files due to size limitations, you may need to download each file individually.

Step 6: Manage and store your exported data. After downloading your data, you can store it on your computer, an external hard drive, or a cloud storage service. Organize your exported files in a way that makes them easy to access and reference in the future. Consider creating a backup copy of your exported data in a different location to ensure its safety.

Step 7: Use your exported data. You can now use your exported data as needed. For example, you can import your emails into another email service, upload your photos to a different cloud storage service, or review your browsing history. If you're transferring data to another service, refer to that service's import instructions to complete the transfer.

Step 8: Regularly update your exports. To keep your backups current, consider setting a regular schedule for exporting your data using Google Takeout. This ensures that you always have the most recent copies of your data.

Step 9: Explore advanced options. Google Takeout offers advanced options for specific services. For instance, you can choose specific albums to export from Google Photos or select individual calendars from Google Calendar. Explore these options to tailor your export to your specific needs.

Step 10: Understand data format and compatibility. Be aware of the formats in which your data is exported. Google Takeout typically exports data in standard formats (e.g., .json, .csv, .mbox) that are compatible with many applications. Ensure that you have the appropriate software to open and use these files.

Google Cloud Storage

Google Cloud Storage is a powerful, scalable, and secure object storage service provided by Google Cloud Platform (GCP). It is designed to handle a wide variety of storage needs, from personal data backup to enterprise-level data storage and management.

How to Use Google Cloud Storage

Step 1: Access Google Cloud Console. Start by navigating to the Google Cloud Console at console.cloud.google.com. Sign in with your Google Workspace or personal Google account. If you don't already have a Google Cloud account, you'll need to create one.

Step 2: Create a new project. In the Google Cloud Console, click on the project dropdown at the top of the screen and select "New Project." Enter a project name, select your billing account, and click "Create." Your new project will be created, and you can now manage resources within it.

Step 3: Enable the Cloud Storage API. To use Google Cloud Storage, you need to enable the Cloud Storage API for your project. In the left-hand menu, navigate to "APIs & Services" > "Library." Search for "Cloud Storage" and click on it, then click "Enable."

Step 4: Create a storage bucket. Buckets are the basic containers in Google Cloud Storage that hold your data. In the left-hand menu, navigate to "Storage" > "Browser." Click "Create bucket" and follow the prompts to configure your bucket settings:

- **Name your bucket**: Enter a unique name for your bucket.
- **Choose a storage class**: Select a storage class based on your needs (e.g., Standard, Nearline, Coldline, Archive).
- **Set location type**: Choose between multi-region, dual-region, or region to determine where your data will be stored.
- **Configure access control**: Choose how to control access to your bucket (e.g., Uniform, Fine-grained).

Step 5: Upload files to your bucket. Once your bucket is created, you can start uploading files. Click on your bucket name to open it, then click "Upload files" or "Upload folder." Select the files or folders from your computer and click "Open" to upload them to your bucket. You can also drag and drop files directly into the bucket in the browser.

Step 6: Manage your files. Google Cloud Storage allows you to organize your files within buckets using folders. Create new folders by clicking the "Create folder" button and naming your folder. Move files into folders by dragging and dropping them or using the "Move" option in the file's context menu.

Step 7: Set up access control. To manage who can access your files, use Identity and Access Management (IAM) policies. In the left-hand menu, navigate to "IAM & Admin" > "IAM." Add members to your project and assign them roles (e.g., Viewer, Editor, Storage Admin). You can also set up bucket and object-level permissions by navigating to your bucket, selecting "Permissions," and configuring the access control settings.

Step 8: Use versioning and lifecycle management. Enable object versioning to keep multiple versions of an object in the same bucket. Go to your bucket settings, click "Enable Object Versioning," and save the changes. Configure lifecycle rules to automatically manage your objects, such as deleting old versions or transitioning them to a different storage class. Navigate to your bucket, click "Lifecycle," and create a new rule.

Step 9: Access your data programmatically. Google Cloud Storage can be accessed programmatically using the Cloud Storage client libraries, REST APIs, or command-line tools like gsutil. Set up the Google Cloud SDK on your local machine by following the installation instructions at cloud.google.com/sdk. Authenticate with your project using gcloud init and start using gsutil to manage your storage from the command line.

Step 10: Monitor and manage usage. Keep track of your storage usage and costs by navigating to "Billing" in the Google Cloud Console. Use the "Reports" and "Budgets & alerts" sections to monitor your expenses and set up alerts for cost thresholds. Additionally, use the "Activity" and "Logs" sections to review actions taken in your storage buckets.

Step 11: Ensure data security and compliance. Google Cloud Storage offers various security features to protect your data. Enable encryption for your data at rest and in transit. Use the "Security" settings to configure encryption keys, audit logging, and access monitoring. Ensure compliance with industry standards and regulations by regularly reviewing and updating your security policies.

Google Docs

Google Docs is a powerful, cloud-based word processing tool that allows you to create, edit, and collaborate on documents in real-time. It is a core part of Google Workspace and offers a wide range of features to enhance productivity and collaboration.

Step 1: To begin, access Google Docs by visiting docs.google.com or by opening the Google Docs app on your mobile device. Sign in with your Google Workspace or personal Google account.

Step 2: Once you're signed in, you'll be taken to the main Google Docs interface. Here, you can see any documents you've previously created or been shared on the main dashboard. To create a new document, click on the "+" (plus) icon labeled "Blank" or select a template from the template gallery.

Step 3: Name your document by clicking on the "Untitled document" field at the top left of the page and typing in your desired title. This will help you easily identify your document in Google Drive later.

Creating and Editing Documents

Step 1: Start typing your content directly into the blank document. Google Docs automatically saves your work as you type, so you never have to worry about losing your progress.

Step 2: Use the toolbar at the top of the page to format your text. You can change the font, size, and color, apply bold, italic, underline, and strikethrough, and adjust alignment and line spacing. Highlight text and use the dropdown menus and icons to apply these formatting options.

Step 3: To insert images, tables, charts, and other elements, click on the "Insert" menu. Choose the type of element you want to add and follow the prompts to insert it into your document. For example, to insert an image, select "Image," then choose to upload from your computer, Google Drive, or search the web.

Step 4: Use the "Tools" menu to access additional features such as spell check, word count, voice typing, and more. These tools can help you enhance the quality and accuracy of your document.

Collaboration Features

Step 1: Share your document with others by clicking the "Share" button in the top right corner. Enter the email addresses of the people you want to share with, and set their permissions to Viewer, Commenter, or Editor. Click "Send" to share the document.

Step 2: Collaborate in real-time. Once your document is shared, multiple people can work on it simultaneously. Each person's cursor is highlighted in a different color, and you can see their changes as they happen.

Step 3: Use the comment feature to leave feedback. Highlight the text you want to comment on, then click the comment icon or right-click and select "Comment." Type your comment and click "Comment" to add it. Collaborators can reply to comments and resolve them when addressed.

Step 4: Suggest edits by switching to "Suggesting" mode. Click on the pencil icon in the top right corner and select "Suggesting." As you make changes, they will appear as suggestions that can be accepted or rejected by the document owner or other editors.

Advanced Features

Step 1: Use the "Explore" feature to enhance your document with additional information. Click on the "Explore" icon in the bottom right corner or go to "Tools" > "Explore." This tool allows you to search the web, find images, and access related documents without leaving Google Docs.

Step 2: Use add-ons to extend the functionality of Google Docs. Click on "Add-ons" in the menu bar and select "Get add-ons." Browse the available add-ons and install the ones that meet your needs. Popular add-ons include grammar checkers, citation managers, and document signing tools.

Step 3: Create and edit documents offline. Enable offline mode by clicking on the menu (three horizontal lines) in the top left corner, selecting "Settings," and toggling on "Offline." This allows you to work on your documents without an internet connection, and changes will sync when you're back online.

Managing Documents

Step 1: Organize your documents by creating folders in Google Drive. Go to drive.google.com, click "New," and select "Folder." Name your folder and click "Create." Drag and drop your Google Docs into the appropriate folders to keep your files organized.

Step 2: Use the search bar at the top of Google Drive or Google Docs to quickly find specific documents. Enter keywords, document titles, or the names of collaborators to locate your files.

Step 3: Set document permissions and access levels by clicking the "Share" button in your document. Adjust the settings to control who can view, comment, or edit your document. You can also set expiration dates for access permissions.

Step 4: Keep track of document changes with version history. Go to "File" > "Version history" > "See version history." This allows you to view and restore previous versions of your document, showing who made changes and when.

Editing

Real-time editing is one of the standout features of Google Docs, enabling multiple users to work on the same document simultaneously. This feature is invaluable for collaboration, allowing team members to make changes, leave comments, and see each other's edits in real-time.

Getting Started with Real-Time Editing

Step 1: Open Google Docs. Start by logging into your Google Workspace or personal Google account at docs.google.com. Open the document you want to collaborate on or create a new one.

Step 2: Share the document. To enable real-time editing, you need to share the document with your collaborators. Click the "Share" button in the top right corner of the screen. Enter the email addresses of the people you want to collaborate with and set their permissions to Viewer, Commenter, or Editor. Click "Send" to invite them.

Step 3: Collaborators join the document. Once your collaborators receive the invitation, they can click the link in the email to open the document. They will appear as colored cursors in the document, each with a unique color to distinguish them.

Working Together in Real-Time

Step 1: See real-time edits. As you and your collaborators work on the document, you can see each other's changes in real-time. Text additions, deletions, and formatting changes appear instantly. Each collaborator's cursor is highlighted in a different color, making it easy to see who is making which edits.

Step 2: Communicate through comments. Use the comment feature to discuss specific parts of the document without altering the text. Highlight the text you want to comment on, click the comment icon, and type your comment. Collaborators can reply to comments, creating a threaded discussion. Once the issue is resolved, you can mark the comment as resolved to keep the document tidy.

Step 3: Suggest edits. If you want to propose changes without making permanent edits, switch to "Suggesting" mode by clicking the pencil icon in the top right corner and selecting "Suggesting." Your changes will appear as suggestions, which can be accepted or rejected by the document owner or other editors. This is useful for making non-intrusive edits and getting approval before finalizing changes.

Step 4: Use chat for quick communication. If multiple collaborators are viewing the document simultaneously, you can use the built-in chat feature to communicate quickly. Click on the chat icon in the top right corner to open a chat window and discuss changes or ask questions without leaving the document.

Managing and Finalizing Edits

Step 1: Track changes with version history. Google Docs automatically saves versions of your document as changes are made. To view the version history, go to "File" > "Version history" > "See version history." This allows you to see who made changes and when, and you can restore previous versions if needed. This is helpful for keeping track of major revisions and ensuring that you can revert to earlier drafts if necessary.

Step 2: Resolve and close comments. As comments are addressed, mark them as resolved to keep the document organized. This helps you keep track of what has been reviewed and ensures that no feedback is overlooked. You can always view resolved comments later if needed.

Step 3: Finalize the document. Once all edits and suggestions have been reviewed and incorporated, switch back to "Editing" mode and make any final adjustments. Ensure that the document is polished and ready for its intended use. Review the document one last time to catch any remaining errors or inconsistencies.

Step 4: Share the final version. When the document is complete, you can share the final version with the intended audience. Adjust the sharing settings if necessary to restrict editing access and ensure that viewers only see the final, polished document.

Templates and Design

Google Docs offers a variety of templates and design tools that help you create professional-looking documents quickly and easily. Whether you need a resume, a business letter, a project proposal, or a newsletter, Google Docs has templates that can save you time and ensure consistency.

Step 1: Open Google Docs. Start by logging into your Google Workspace or personal Google account at docs.google.com.

Step 2: Access the template gallery. On the main Google Docs dashboard, you will see the "Template Gallery" at the top. Click on "Template Gallery" to view all available templates.

Step 3: Choose a template. Browse through the template categories such as Resumes, Letters, Education, Work, and more. Click on the template that best suits your needs. This will open a new document based on the selected template.

Step 4: Customize the template. Once the template is open, you can start customizing it to fit your specific needs. Click on any text or image in the template to edit it. Replace placeholder text with your own content, change fonts and colors, and adjust the layout as needed.

Step 5: Save your customized template. Google Docs automatically saves your changes as you work. However, you can also rename the document by clicking on the title at the top and typing a new name. This will help you easily find and organize your customized templates in Google Drive.

Design Your Document

Step 1: Utilize the formatting tools. Use the toolbar at the top of the page to format your text and design elements. You can change the font, size, and color, apply bold, italic, underline, and strikethrough, and adjust alignment and line spacing. Highlight the text you want to format and use the dropdown menus and icons to apply these formatting options.

Step 2: Insert images and graphics. To add visual elements to your document, click on the "Insert" menu and select "Image." You can upload images from your computer, search the web, or choose from your Google Drive or Google Photos. Once inserted, you can resize and position the images as needed.

Step 3: Use tables for structured content. If you need to organize information in a structured format, insert a table by clicking on the "Table" menu and selecting the number of rows and columns you need. You can customize the table's appearance by adjusting cell sizes, adding borders, and changing background colors.

Step 4: Add headers and footers. To give your document a professional look, add headers and footers. Click on the "Insert" menu and select "Header" or "Footer." You can include page numbers, dates, titles, or any other relevant information. Use the formatting tools to style the header or footer as desired.

Step 5: Apply document styles. Google Docs provides predefined styles for headings, subtitles, and normal text to ensure consistency throughout your document. Highlight the text you want to style, then click on the "Styles" dropdown menu in the toolbar and choose the appropriate style. You can customize these styles by modifying the font, size, and color.

Step 6: Use the "Explore" feature for design inspiration. The "Explore" feature can help you find relevant images, documents, and content to enhance your document's design. Click on the "Explore" icon in the bottom right corner or go to "Tools" > "Explore." Search for topics related to your document to find useful resources and design ideas.

Step 7: Create your own template. If you frequently use a particular layout or design, consider creating your own template. Design your document as usual, then save it as a template. To do this, click on "File" > "Make a copy" and save the document with a new name. You can use this copy as a template for future documents by editing and saving new versions.

Google Sheets

Google Sheets is a versatile, cloud-based spreadsheet application that is part of Google Workspace. It allows you to create, edit, and collaborate on spreadsheets online, making it a powerful tool for data analysis, financial planning, project management, and more.

Getting Started with Google Sheets

Step 1: To begin using Google Sheets, access it by visiting sheets.google.com in your web browser or by opening the Google Sheets app on your mobile device. Sign in with your Google Workspace or personal Google account.

Step 2: Once signed in, you will be taken to the main Google Sheets interface. Here, you will see any spreadsheets you have previously created or shared with you displayed on the main dashboard. To create a new spreadsheet, click on the "+" (plus) icon labeled "Blank" or select a template from the template gallery.

Step 3: After creating a new spreadsheet, you should name it by clicking on the "Untitled spreadsheet" field at the top left of the page and typing in your desired title. This will help you easily identify your spreadsheet in Google Drive later.

How to Create and Edit Spreadsheets

Step 1: Start entering your data directly into the cells of the blank spreadsheet. Google Sheets automatically saves your work as you type, so you never have to worry about losing your progress.

Step 2: Use the toolbar at the top of the page to format your data. You can change the font, size, and color, apply bold, italic, underline, and strikethrough, and adjust alignment and cell borders. Highlight the cells you want to format and use the dropdown menus and icons to apply these formatting options.

Step 3: To insert additional elements such as charts, images, or functions, click on the "Insert" menu. Choose the type of element you want to add and follow the prompts to insert it into your spreadsheet. For example, to insert a chart, select "Chart," and choose the type of chart that best represents your data.

Step 4: Use the "Data" menu to sort and filter your data. Highlight the range of cells you want to sort or filter, then click "Data" and select the appropriate option. Sorting and filtering help you organize and analyze your data more effectively.

Formulas and Functions

Step 1: Google Sheets supports a wide range of formulas and functions that allow you to perform calculations and data analysis. To enter a formula, click on a cell, type "=" followed by the formula (e.g., "=SUM(A1

)"), and press Enter. The result of the formula will be displayed in the cell.

Step 2: Explore the function library by clicking on the "Insert" menu and selecting "Function." Browse the categories or use the search bar to find the function you need. Common functions include SUM, AVERAGE, COUNT, IF, and VLOOKUP.

Step 3: Use cell references in your formulas to perform calculations across different cells and ranges. For example, "=A1+B1" adds the values in cells A1 and B1. You can also use absolute and relative references to control how formulas update when copied to other cells.

Collaboration and Sharing

Step 1: Share your spreadsheet with others by clicking the "Share" button in the top right corner. Enter the email addresses of the people you want to share with, and set their permissions to Viewer, Commenter, or Editor. Click "Send" to share the spreadsheet.

Step 2: Collaborate in real-time. Once your spreadsheet is shared, multiple people can work on it simultaneously. Each person's cursor is highlighted in a different color, and you can see their changes as they happen.

Step 3: Use the comment feature to discuss specific parts of the spreadsheet without altering the data. Click on a cell, then click the comment icon or right-click and select "Comment." Type your comment and click "Comment" to add it. Collaborators can reply to comments and resolve them when addressed.

Managing Your Spreadsheets

Step 1: Organize your spreadsheets by creating folders in Google Drive. Go to drive.google.com, click "New," and select "Folder." Name your folder and click "Create." Drag and drop your Google Sheets into the appropriate folders to keep your files organized.

Step 2: Use the search bar at the top of Google Drive or Google Sheets to quickly find specific spreadsheets. Enter keywords, spreadsheet titles, or the names of collaborators to locate your files.

Step 3: Set spreadsheet permissions and access levels by clicking the "Share" button in your spreadsheet. Adjust the settings to control who can view, comment, or edit your spreadsheet. You can also set expiration dates for access permissions.

Step 4: Keep track of changes with version history. Go to "File" > "Version history" > "See version history." This allows you to view and restore previous versions of your spreadsheet, showing who made changes and when.

Data Management

Google Sheets is an excellent tool for managing and analyzing data. With its robust features, you can efficiently organize, manipulate, and visualize your data.

Importing and Exporting Data

Step 1: Importing Data. To import data into Google Sheets, start by opening your spreadsheet and clicking on "File" > "Import." You can choose to upload a file from your computer, select a file from your Google Drive, or import data from a URL. Supported file formats include .csv, .tsv, .txt, .xlsx, and more. Follow the prompts to select your file and choose how you want to import the data (e.g., create a new spreadsheet, insert new sheet(s), replace current sheet, etc.).

Step 2: Exporting Data. To export your data from Google Sheets, click on "File" > "Download." You can download your spreadsheet in various formats such as Microsoft Excel (.xlsx), OpenDocument (.ods), PDF, CSV, TSV, and more. Select the desired format and the file will be downloaded to your computer.

Organizing Data

Step 1: Sorting Data. To sort data in Google Sheets, highlight the range of cells you want to sort. Click on "Data" > "Sort range." You can choose to sort by specific columns and specify whether you want to sort in ascending or descending order. Sorting helps you organize your data logically and makes it easier to analyze.

Step 2: Filtering Data. Filters allow you to display only the data that meets certain criteria. To apply a filter, highlight the range of cells you want to filter, then click on "Data" > "Create a filter." Small filter icons will appear in the column headers. Click on a filter icon to set your filtering criteria. You can filter by values, conditions (e.g., greater than, less than), or search for specific data.

Step 3: Using Conditional Formatting. Conditional formatting changes the appearance of cells based on their values. To apply conditional formatting, highlight the range of cells, then click on "Format" > "Conditional formatting." Set the formatting rules based on conditions such as text contains, cell is empty, greater than, etc. Choose the formatting style (e.g., background color, text color) and click "Done." This helps highlight important data and identify trends.

Analyzing Data

Step 1: Using Functions and Formulas. Google Sheets provides a wide range of functions and formulas to perform calculations and analyze data. Common functions include SUM, AVERAGE, COUNT, MAX, MIN, IF, and VLOOKUP. To enter a formula, click on a cell, type "=" followed by the formula (e.g., "=SUM(A1

)"), and press Enter. Use cell references to perform calculations across different cells and ranges.

Step 2: Creating Pivot Tables. Pivot tables are powerful tools for summarizing and analyzing large datasets. To create a pivot table, highlight the range of data, then click on "Data" > "Pivot table." In the pivot table editor, drag and drop fields into the Rows, Columns, Values, and Filters sections to organize and summarize your data. Pivot tables help you quickly identify patterns and insights.

Step 3: Visualizing Data with Charts. Charts provide a visual representation of your data. To create a chart, highlight the data range, then click on "Insert" > "Chart." In the chart editor, choose the type of chart (e.g., bar, line, pie, scatter) and customize its appearance. Adjust the chart's settings, such as titles, labels, and colors, to make it clear and informative. Charts help you communicate your data effectively.

Data Validation

Step 1: Applying Data Validation. Data validation ensures that the data entered into cells meets specific criteria. To apply data validation, highlight the range of cells, then click on "Data" > "Data validation." Set the criteria (e.g., list of items, number, text, date) and specify the validation rule (e.g., whole number between 1 and 10). Click "Save" to apply the validation. This helps maintain data integrity and accuracy.

Step 2: Protecting Sheets and Ranges. To protect your data from unauthorized changes, you can protect entire sheets or specific ranges. Click on "Data" > "Protected sheets and ranges." Select the range or sheet you want to protect and set the permissions. You can allow certain users to edit the protected range while restricting others. This ensures that critical data remains secure.

Automating Tasks

Step 1: Using Google Sheets Macros. Macros automate repetitive tasks by recording your actions and replaying them. To create a macro, click on "Extensions" > "Macros" > "Record macro." Perform the actions you want to automate, then click "Save" and name your macro. To run the macro, click on "Extensions" > "Macros" and select the macro you created.

Step 2: Writing Custom Scripts with Google Apps Script. For more advanced automation, you can write custom scripts using Google Apps Script. Click on "Extensions" > "Apps Script" to open the script editor. Write your script using JavaScript and Google Sheets-specific functions. Save and run your script to automate tasks, create custom functions, and integrate with other Google services.

Formulas and Functions

Google Sheets is equipped with a wide range of formulas and functions that allow you to perform complex calculations and data analysis. Mastering these tools can significantly enhance your productivity and enable you to extract valuable insights from your data.

Understanding Formulas and Functions

Formulas are expressions that perform calculations on data in your spreadsheet. They start with an equal sign (=) followed by the calculation to be performed.

Functions are predefined formulas that simplify complex calculations. Google Sheets offers a variety of functions for different purposes, such as mathematical, statistical, logical, and text functions.

Basic Formulas and Functions

Step 1: Entering a Formula. To enter a formula, click on the cell where you want the result to appear, type "=" followed by the expression you want to calculate. For example, to add the values in cells A1 and B1, type "=A1+B1" and press Enter. The result will appear in the selected cell.

Step 2: Using the SUM Function. The SUM function adds a range of cells. To use it, click on the cell where you want the result to appear, type "=SUM(" followed by the range of cells you want to add. For example, to sum the values in cells A1 to A10, type "=SUM(A1

)" and press Enter.

Step 3: Using the AVERAGE Function. The AVERAGE function calculates the mean of a range of cells. Click on the cell where you want the result, type "=AVERAGE(" followed by the range of cells. For example, "=AVERAGE(A1

)" calculates the average of values in A1 to A10.

Step 4: Using the MIN and MAX Functions. The MIN function returns the smallest value in a range, while the MAX function returns the largest. To use these functions, type "=MIN(A1

)" or "=MAX(A1
)" and press Enter.

Logical Functions

Step 1: Using the IF Function. The IF function performs a logical test and returns one value if the test is true and another if it is false. To use it, type "=IF(" followed by the condition, the value if true, and the value if false. For example, "=IF(A1>10, "High", "Low")" returns "High" if A1 is greater than 10, otherwise it returns "Low."

Step 2: Using the AND and OR Functions. The AND function returns TRUE if all conditions are met, while the OR function returns TRUE if any condition is met. For example, "=AND(A1>10, B1<5)" returns TRUE if A1 is greater than 10 and B1 is less than 5. "=OR(A1>10, B1<5)" returns TRUE if either condition is met.

Text Functions

Step 1: Using the CONCATENATE Function. The CONCATENATE function combines text from multiple cells into one cell. To use it, type "=CONCATENATE(" followed by the cells you want to combine. For example, "=CONCATENATE(A1, " ", B1)" combines the text in A1 and B1 with a space in between.

Step 2: Using the LEFT, RIGHT, and MID Functions. The LEFT function returns the first character(s) in a text string based on the number of characters you specify. The RIGHT function returns the last character(s), and the MID function returns a specific number of characters from a specified starting position. For example, "=LEFT(A1, 3)" returns the first three characters in A1, "=RIGHT(A1, 2)" returns the last two characters, and "=MID(A1, 2, 3)" returns three characters starting from the second character.

Lookup Functions

Step 1: Using the VLOOKUP Function. The VLOOKUP function searches for a value in the first column of a range and returns a value in the same row from a specified column. To use it, type "=VLOOKUP(" followed by the search key, range, index, and is_sorted. For example, "=VLOOKUP(B1, A2

, 3, FALSE)" searches for the value in B1 in the first column of A2
and returns the value in the third column of the same row.

Step 2: Using the HLOOKUP Function. The HLOOKUP function works like VLOOKUP but searches for a value in the first row of a range and returns a value in the same column from a specified row. For example, "=HLOOKUP(B1, A1

, 3, FALSE)" searches for the value in B1 in the first row of A1
and returns the value in the third row of the same column.

Advanced Functions

Step 1: Using the ARRAYFORMULA Function. The ARRAYFORMULA function applies a formula to a range of cells. For example, "=ARRAYFORMULA(A1

*B1
)" multiplies each cell in the range A1
by the corresponding cell in B1

.

Step 2: Using the IMPORTRANGE Function. The IMPORTRANGE function imports data from another Google Sheets document. To use it, type "=IMPORTRANGE(" followed by the URL of the source sheet and the range to import. For example, "=IMPORTRANGE("https://docs.google.com/spreadsheets/d/abc123", "Sheet1!A1

")" imports the range A1
from Sheet1 of the specified spreadsheet.

Array Functions

Array functions in Google Sheets allow you to perform calculations on a range of cells and return multiple results in a single function call. These functions are powerful tools for data analysis and manipulation, enabling you to work with complex datasets more efficiently.

Understanding Array Functions

Array functions operate on a range of cells and can return multiple values, often across multiple cells. These functions can simplify complex calculations and make it easier to work with large datasets. The primary array functions in Google Sheets include ARRAYFORMULA, FILTER, SORT, and UNIQUE.

Using ARRAY FORMULA

Step 1: Basic Usage. The ARRAYFORMULA function applies a formula to an entire range of cells, rather than a single cell. To use ARRAYFORMULA, type =ARRAYFORMULA(followed by the range and the formula. For example, to multiply each cell in the range A1

by 2, type =ARRAYFORMULA(A1:A10 * 2) and press Enter. The result will be displayed in the corresponding cells in the column where the formula is entered.

Step 2: Applying Functions to a Range. ARRAYFORMULA can also be used to apply other functions to a range of cells. For example, to add the values in columns A and B for rows 1 to 10, type =ARRAYFORMULA(A1:A10 + B1:B10) and press Enter. Each cell in the range will display the sum of the corresponding cells in columns A and B.

Using the FILTER Function

Step 1: Basic Usage. The FILTER function returns an array of values that meet specific criteria. To use FILTER, type =FILTER(followed by the range and the criteria. For example, to filter the range A1

to show only values greater than 5, type =FILTER(A1:A10, A1:A10 > 5) and press Enter. The result will display the filtered values in the column where the formula is entered.

Step 2: Multiple Criteria. The FILTER function can handle multiple criteria. For example, to filter the range A1

to show values greater than 5 and less than 15, type =FILTER(A1:A10, A1:A10 > 5, A1:A10 < 15) and press Enter. The result will display values that meet both criteria.

Using the SORT Function

Step 1: Basic Usage. The SORT function sorts a range of cells based on specified criteria. To use SORT, type =SORT(followed by the range and the sort criteria. For example, to sort the range A1 in ascending order, type =SORT(A1:A10, 1, TRUE) and press Enter. The result will display the sorted values in the column where the formula is entered.

Step 2: Sorting by Multiple Columns. The SORT function can also sort by multiple columns. For example, to sort the range A1

first by column A in ascending order and then by column B in descending order, type =SORT(A1:B10, 1, TRUE, 2, FALSE) and press Enter. The result will display the sorted values in the specified order.

Using the UNIQUE Function

Step 1: Basic Usage. The UNIQUE function returns a list of unique values from a range. To use UNIQUE, type =UNIQUE(followed by the range. For example, to extract unique values from the range A1

, type =UNIQUE(A1:A10) and press Enter. The result will display the unique values in the column where the formula is entered.

Step 2: Unique Combinations. The UNIQUE function can also be used to find unique combinations of values in multiple columns. For example, to find unique combinations of values in the range A1

, type =UNIQUE(A1:B10) and press Enter. The result will display unique pairs of values from the specified range.

Combining Array Functions

Array functions can be combined to perform complex data analysis tasks. For example, to filter unique values from the range A1

that are greater than 5, type =UNIQUE(FILTER(A1:A10, A1:A10 > 5)) and press Enter. The result will display the unique values that meet the specified criteria.

Practical Examples

Example 1: Calculating Sales Tax for Multiple Items. Suppose you have a list of prices in column A and you want to calculate the sales tax (10%) for each item. Type =ARRAYFORMULA(A1:A10 * 0.10) and press Enter. The result will display the sales tax for each item in the corresponding cells.

Example 2: Filtering and Sorting Data. Suppose you have a list of sales figures in column A and you want to display the unique values greater than 50, sorted in descending order. Type =SORT(UNIQUE(FILTER(A1:A10, A1:A10 > 50)), 1, FALSE) and press Enter. The result will display the unique values greater than 50, sorted in descending order.

Google Sheets offers a variety of database functions that allow you to perform complex data queries, aggregations, and filtering directly within your spreadsheet. These functions are similar to SQL queries in their functionality and can be extremely powerful for managing and analyzing large datasets.

Understanding Database Functions

Database functions in Google Sheets are used to query and manipulate data ranges as if they were database tables. The primary database functions include QUERY, FILTER, SORT, and UNIQUE. Each of these functions allows you to interact with your data in advanced ways, making it easier to analyze and extract insights.

Using the QUERY Function

Step 1: Basic Usage. The QUERY function allows you to use SQL-like syntax to query your data. To use QUERY, type =QUERY(followed by the data range, the query string, and optionally, headers. For example, to select all data from the range A1

where the value in column A is greater than 10, type =QUERY(A1:C10, "SELECT * WHERE A > 10") and press Enter. The result will display the filtered data.

Step 2: Advanced Queries. You can perform more complex queries using functions such as SUM, AVG, COUNT, and GROUP BY. For example, to calculate the total sales in column C grouped by the product in column A, type =QUERY(A1:C10, "SELECT A, SUM(C) GROUP BY A") and press Enter. The result will display the total sales for each product.

Using the FILTER Function

Step 1: Basic Usage. The FILTER function returns an array of values that meet specific criteria. To use FILTER, type =FILTER(followed by the data range and the criteria. For example, to filter the range A1

to show only values greater than 5, type =FILTER(A1:A10, A1:A10 > 5) and press Enter. The result will display the filtered values in the column where the formula is entered.

Step 2: Multiple Criteria. The FILTER function can handle multiple criteria. For example, to filter the range A1 to show values greater than 5 and less than 15, type =FILTER(A1:A10, A1:A10 > 5, A1:A10 < 15) and press Enter. The result will display values that meet both criteria.

Using the SORT Function

Step 1: Basic Usage. The SORT function sorts a range of cells based on specified criteria. To use SORT, type =SORT(followed by the data range and the sort criteria. For example, to sort the range A1

in ascending order, type =SORT(A1:A10, 1, TRUE) and press Enter. The result will display the sorted values in the column where the formula is entered.

Step 2: Sorting by Multiple Columns. The SORT function can also sort by multiple columns. For example, to sort the range A1

first by column A in ascending order and then by column B in descending order, type =SORT(A1:B10, 1, TRUE, 2, FALSE) and press Enter. The result will display the sorted values in the specified order.

Using the UNIQUE Function

Step 1: Basic Usage. The UNIQUE function returns a list of unique values from a range. To use UNIQUE, type =UNIQUE(followed by the range. For example, to extract unique values from the range A1

, type =UNIQUE(A1:A10) and press Enter. The result will display the unique values in the column where the formula is entered.

Step 2: Unique Combinations. The UNIQUE function can also be used to find unique combinations of values in multiple columns. For example, to find unique combinations of values in the range A1

, type =UNIQUE(A1:B10) and press Enter. The result will display unique pairs of values from the specified range.

Combining Database Functions

Database functions can be combined to perform complex data analysis tasks. For example, to filter unique values from the range A1

that are greater than 5, type =UNIQUE(FILTER(A1:A10, A1:A10 > 5)) and press Enter. The result will display the unique values that meet the specified criteria.

Practical Examples

Example 1: Calculating Total Sales by Product. Suppose you have a dataset in columns A to C where column A contains product names, column B contains quantities sold, and column C contains sales amounts. To calculate the total sales by product, use the QUERY function: =QUERY(A1:C10, "SELECT A, SUM(C) GROUP BY A"). This will display the total sales for each product.

Example 2: Filtering and Sorting Data. Suppose you have a list of sales figures in column A and you want to display the unique values greater than 50, sorted in descending order. Use the SORT and UNIQUE functions together: =SORT(UNIQUE(FILTER(A1:A10, A1:A10 > 50)), 1, FALSE). This will display the unique values greater than 50, sorted in descending order.

Example 3: Creating a Custom Report. Suppose you have a dataset in columns A to D where column A contains dates, column B contains product names, column C contains quantities sold, and column D contains sales amounts. You want to create a report showing total sales by product for a specific date range. Use the QUERY function: =QUERY(A1:D10, "SELECT B, SUM(D) WHERE A >= DATE '2025-01-01' AND A <= DATE '2025-12-31' GROUP BY B"). This will display the total sales by product for the specified date range.

Math Functions

Google Sheets provides a comprehensive set of math functions that allow you to perform a wide range of mathematical operations and calculations. These functions are essential for data analysis, financial modeling, statistical analysis, and various other applications.

Basic Math Functions

Step 1: Using the SUM Function. The SUM function adds a range of cells. To use it, click on the cell where you want the result to appear, type =SUM(followed by the range of cells you want to add. For example, to sum the values in cells A1 to A10, type =SUM(A1:A10) and press Enter. The result will be displayed in the selected cell.

Step 2: Using the AVERAGE Function. The AVERAGE function calculates the mean of a range of cells. Click on the cell where you want the result, type =AVERAGE(followed by the range of cells. For example, =AVERAGE(A1:A10) calculates the average of values in A1 to A10.

Step 3: Using the MIN and MAX Functions. The MIN function returns the smallest value in a range, while the MAX function returns the largest. To use these functions, type =MIN(A1:A10) or =MAX(A1:A10) and press Enter. The result will display the smallest or largest value in the specified range.

Step 4: Using the COUNT Function. The COUNT function counts the number of cells that contain numbers in a range. Type =COUNT(followed by the range of cells. For example, =COUNT(A1:A10) counts the number of cells in A1 to A10 that contain numbers.

Advanced Math Functions

Step 1: Using the ROUND, ROUNDUP, and ROUNDDOWN Functions. These functions round numbers to a specified number of decimal places.

- To round a number, use =ROUND(number, num_digits). For example, =ROUND(A1, 2) rounds the value in A1 to two decimal places.
- To always round up, use =ROUNDUP(number, num_digits). For example, =ROUNDUP(A1, 2) always rounds up the value in A1 to two decimal places.
- To always round down, use =ROUNDDOWN(number, num_digits). For example, =ROUNDDOWN(A1, 2) always rounds down the value in A1 to two decimal places.

Step 2: Using the SQRT Function. The SQRT function returns the square root of a number. Type =SQRT(followed by the number or cell reference. For example, =SQRT(A1) calculates the square root of the value in cell A1.

Step 3: Using the POWER Function. The POWER function raises a number to a specified power. Type =POWER(followed by the number and the exponent. For example, =POWER(A1, 2) raises the value in cell A1 to the power of 2 (squares it).

Step 4: Using the ABS Function. The ABS function returns the absolute value of a number. Type =ABS(followed by the number or cell reference. For example, =ABS(A1) returns the absolute value of the number in cell A1.

Trigonometric Functions

Step 1: Using the SIN, COS, and TAN Functions. These functions return the sine, cosine, and tangent of an angle, respectively. The angle must be in radians.

- To calculate the sine of an angle, use =SIN(angle). For example, =SIN(A1) calculates the sine of the angle in cell A1.
- To calculate the cosine of an angle, use =COS(angle). For example, =COS(A1) calculates the cosine of the angle in cell A1.
- To calculate the tangent of an angle, use =TAN(angle). For example, =TAN(A1) calculates the tangent of the angle in cell A1.

Step 2: Using the RADIANS and DEGREES Functions. These functions convert angles between degrees and radians.

- To convert an angle from degrees to radians, use =RADIANS(degrees). For example, =RADIANS(180) converts 180 degrees to radians.
- To convert an angle from radians to degrees, use =DEGREES(radians). For example, =DEGREES(PI()) converts π radians to degrees.

Logarithmic and Exponential Functions

Step 1: Using the LOG and LN Functions. The LOG function returns the logarithm of a number with a specified base, and the LN function returns the natural logarithm (base e) of a number.

- To calculate the logarithm of a number with a specific base, use =LOG(number, base). For example, =LOG(A1, 10) calculates the base 10 logarithm of the value in cell A1.
- To calculate the natural logarithm of a number, use =LN(number). For example, =LN(A1) calculates the natural logarithm of the value in cell A1.

Step 2: Using the EXP Function. The EXP function returns e raised to the power of a given number. Type =EXP(number). For example, =EXP(A1) calculates e raised to the power of the value in cell A1.

Practical Examples

Example 1: Calculating Compound Interest. To calculate the compound interest for a principal amount P, interest rate r, and time t, use the formula =P*(1+r)^t. For example, if P is in cell A1, r in B1, and t in C1, the formula would be =A1*(1+B1)^C1.

Example 2: Using Trigonometric Functions in Geometry. To calculate the hypotenuse of a right-angled triangle with sides a and b, use the Pythagorean theorem: =SQRT(A1^2 + B1^2). If a and b are in cells A1 and B1, respectively, this formula will give the hypotenuse.

Example 3: Converting Temperatures from Celsius to Fahrenheit. Use the formula =A1*9/5 + 32 to convert a temperature in Celsius (in cell A1) to Fahrenheit.

Engineering Functions

Google Sheets provides a variety of engineering functions designed to assist with complex calculations and data analysis commonly used in engineering tasks. These functions are powerful tools that can handle a range of engineering problems, from unit conversions to advanced mathematical computations.

Basic Engineering Functions

Step 1: Using the CONVERT Function. The CONVERT function allows you to convert a number from one unit of measurement to another. To use CONVERT, type =CONVERT(followed by the value, the unit to convert from, and the unit to convert to. For example, to convert 10 meters to feet, type =CONVERT(10, "m", "ft") and press Enter. The result will display the converted value.

Step 2: Using the BESSEL Functions. The BESSEL functions calculate Bessel functions, which are important in various fields of engineering and physics. Google Sheets includes several BESSEL functions, such as BESSELI, BESSELJ, BESSELK, and BESSELY.

- BESSELI: Calculates the modified Bessel function of the first kind. Use =BESSELI(x, n) where x is the value and n is the order.
- BESSELJ: Calculates the Bessel function of the first kind. Use =BESSELJ(x, n) where x is the value and n is the order.
- BESSELK: Calculates the modified Bessel function of the second kind. Use =BESSELK(x, n) where x is the value and n is the order.
- BESSELY: Calculates the Bessel function of the second kind. Use =BESSELY(x, n) where x is the value and n is the order.

Step 3: Using the COMPLEX Function. The COMPLEX function creates a complex number from real and imaginary coefficients. To use COMPLEX, type =COMPLEX(real, imaginary, [suffix]). For example, =COMPLEX(3, 4, "i") creates the complex number 3 + 4i.

Step 4: Using the IM Functions. Google Sheets includes several functions to handle complex numbers, such as IMABS, IMAGINARY, IMREAL, and IMSUM.

- IMABS: Returns the absolute value of a complex number. Use =IMABS(complex_number).
- IMAGINARY: Returns the imaginary coefficient of a complex number. Use =IMAGINARY(complex_number).
- IMREAL: Returns the real coefficient of a complex number. Use =IMREAL(complex_number).
- IMSUM: Adds multiple complex numbers. Use =IMSUM(complex_number1, complex_number2, ...).

Advanced Engineering Functions

Step 1: Using the DELTA Function. The DELTA function tests whether two values are equal. It returns 1 if the values are equal and 0 otherwise. To use DELTA, type =DELTA(number1, [number2]). For example, =DELTA(5, 5) returns 1 because the values are equal.

Step 2: Using the ERF and ERFC Functions. The ERF function returns the error function, while the ERFC function returns the complementary error function.

- ERF: To use, type =ERF(lower_limit, [upper_limit]). For example, =ERF(1) returns the error function of 1.
- ERFC: To use, type =ERFC(x). For example, =ERFC(1) returns the complementary error function of 1.

Step 3: Using the GAMMALN Function. The GAMMALN function returns the natural logarithm of the gamma function. To use GAMMALN, type =GAMMALN(x). For example, =GAMMALN(5) returns the natural logarithm of the gamma function of 5.

Step 4: Using the PI Function. The PI function returns the value of π (pi). To use PI, simply type =PI(). This function is useful for various engineering calculations involving circles and trigonometry.

Step 5: Using the GCD and LCM Functions. The GCD function returns the greatest common divisor, while the LCM function returns the least common multiple.

- GCD: To use, type =GCD(number1, number2, ...). For example, =GCD(12, 8) returns 4.
- LCM: To use, type =LCM(number1, number2, ...). For example, =LCM(4, 5) returns 20.

Practical Examples

Example 1: Converting Units. Suppose you need to convert 50 kilometers to miles. Use the CONVERT function: =CONVERT(50, "km", "mi"). This will return the value in miles.

Example 2: Working with Complex Numbers. To add two complex numbers, 3 + 4i and 1 + 2i, use the IMSUM function: =IMSUM(COMPLEX(3, 4), COMPLEX(1, 2)). This will return the sum of the complex numbers.

Example 3: Calculating Bessel Functions. To calculate the Bessel function of the first kind for x = 3 and n = 2, use the BESSELJ function: =BESSELJ(3, 2). This will return the Bessel function value.

Example 4: Finding the Greatest Common Divisor. To find the GCD of 56 and 98, use the GCD function: =GCD(56, 98). This will return the greatest common divisor.

Filter functions in Google Sheets are powerful tools that enable you to extract and display specific data based on criteria you define. These functions help you manage large datasets by isolating relevant information, making data analysis more efficient and effective.

Using the FILTER Function

The FILTER function in Google Sheets allows you to filter a range of data based on specific criteria.

Step 1: Basic Usage. To use the FILTER function, type =FILTER(followed by the range of data you want to filter and the criteria for filtering. For example, to filter the range A1

to show only values greater than 5, type =FILTER(A1:A10, A1:A10 > 5) and press Enter. The result will display the filtered values in the column where the formula is entered.

Step 2: Multiple Criteria. The FILTER function can handle multiple criteria. For example, to filter the range A1

to show values greater than 5 and less than 15, type =FILTER(A1:A10, A1:A10 > 5, A1:A10 < 15) and press Enter. The result will display values that meet both criteria.

Step 3: Filtering Multiple Columns. You can also filter data based on criteria in multiple columns. For example, to filter rows where the values in column A are greater than 5 and the values in column B are less than 10, type =FILTER(A1:B10, A1:A10 > 5, B1:B10 < 10) and press Enter.

Combining the SORT and FILTER functions allows you to sort the filtered data.

Step 1: Basic Sorting. To sort filtered data, nest the FILTER function within the SORT function. For example, to filter the range A1

to show values greater than 5 and then sort them in ascending order, type =SORT(FILTER(A1:A10, A1:A10 > 5), 1, TRUE) and press Enter. The result will display the filtered and sorted values.

Step 2: Sorting by Multiple Columns. To sort filtered data by multiple columns, use the SORT function with multiple column indices. For example, to filter rows where column A values are greater than 5 and then sort by column B in descending order, type =SORT(FILTER(A1:B10, A1:A10 > 5), 2, FALSE) and press Enter.

Using the UNIQUE Function with FILTER

Combining the UNIQUE and FILTER functions allows you to filter data and remove duplicates.

Step 1: Basic Filtering and Removing Duplicates. To filter the range A1

to show values greater than 5 and remove duplicates, type =UNIQUE(FILTER(A1:A10, A1:A10 > 5)) and press Enter. The result will display the filtered and unique values.

Step 2: Filtering and Removing Duplicates Across Multiple Columns. To filter rows based on criteria and remove duplicates across multiple columns, use the UNIQUE function with the FILTER function. For example, to filter rows where column A values are greater than 5 and remove duplicate rows, type =UNIQUE(FILTER(A1:B10, A1:A10 > 5)) and press Enter.

Using the QUERY Function for Advanced Filtering

The QUERY function provides more advanced filtering capabilities using SQL-like syntax.

Step 1: Basic Usage. To use the QUERY function, type =QUERY(followed by the data range, the query string, and optionally, headers. For example, to select all data from the range A1

where the value in column A is greater than 10, type =QUERY(A1:C10, "SELECT * WHERE A > 10") and press Enter. The result will display the filtered data.

Step 2: Advanced Queries. The QUERY function allows for more complex queries using functions such as SUM, AVG, COUNT, and GROUP BY. For example, to calculate the total sales in column C grouped by the product in column A, type =QUERY(A1:C10, "SELECT A, SUM(C) GROUP BY A") and press Enter. The result will display the total sales for each product.

Practical Examples

Example 1: Filtering Sales Data. Suppose you have a dataset in columns A to C where column A contains product names, column B contains sales quantities, and column C contains sales amounts. To filter the rows where sales quantities are greater than 50, use the FILTER function: =FILTER(A1:C10, B1:B10 > 50). This will display only the rows with sales quantities greater than 50.

Example 2: Sorting and Filtering Employee Data. Suppose you have employee data in columns A to D where column A contains names, column B contains departments, column C contains salaries, and column D contains hire dates. To filter employees in the "Sales" department and sort them by salary in descending order, use the SORT and FILTER functions: =SORT(FILTER(A1:D10, B1:B10 = "Sales"), 3, FALSE). This will display the filtered and sorted employee data.

Example 3: Removing Duplicate Entries in Customer Data. Suppose you have a list of customer names in column A and you want to remove duplicates. To filter out customers who have placed more than one order and display unique names, use the UNIQUE and FILTER functions: =UNIQUE(FILTER(A1:A10, A1:A10 <> "")). This will display the unique customer names.

Financial Functions

Google Sheets offers a comprehensive suite of financial functions that enable you to perform various financial calculations, such as loan payments, interest rates, investment valuations, and depreciation. These functions are essential for financial analysis, budgeting, forecasting, and other financial planning tasks.

Basic Financial Functions

Step 1: Using the PMT Function. The PMT function calculates the periodic payment for an annuity based on constant periodic payments and a constant interest rate. To use PMT, type =PMT(rate, nper, pv, [fv], [type]). For example, to calculate the monthly payment on a loan with an annual interest rate of 5%, a term of 30 years, and a principal amount of $200,000, type =PMT(5%/12, 30*12, -200000) and press Enter. The result will display the monthly payment amount.

Step 2: Using the FV Function. The FV (Future Value) function calculates the future value of an investment based on periodic, constant payments and a constant interest rate. To use FV, type =FV(rate, nper, pmt, [pv], [type]). For example, to calculate the future value of an investment with an annual interest rate of 6%, monthly payments of $100, and a term of 20 years, type =FV(6%/12, 20*12, -100) and press Enter. The result will display the future value of the investment.

Step 3: Using the PV Function. The PV (Present Value) function calculates the present value of an investment or loan based on periodic, constant payments and a constant interest rate. To use PV, type =PV(rate, nper, pmt, [fv], [type]). For example, to calculate the present value of an investment with an annual interest rate of 4%, monthly payments of $150, and a term of 10 years, type =PV(4%/12, 10*12, -150) and press Enter. The result will display the present value of the investment.

Step 4: Using the RATE Function. The RATE function calculates the interest rate per period of an annuity. To use RATE, type =RATE(nper, pmt, pv, [fv], [type], [guess]). For example, to calculate the interest rate of a loan with 60 monthly payments of $500 and a principal amount of $25,000, type =RATE(60, -500, 25000) and press Enter. The result will display the monthly interest rate.

Step 5: Using the NPER Function. The NPER function calculates the number of periods for an investment based on periodic, constant payments and a constant interest rate. To use NPER, type =NPER(rate, pmt, pv, [fv], [type]). For example, to calculate the number of monthly payments needed to repay a loan with an annual interest rate of 7%, monthly payments of $400, and a principal amount of $10,000, type =NPER(7%/12, -400, 10000) and press Enter. The result will display the number of periods.

Advanced Financial Functions

Step 1: Using the IRR Function. The IRR (Internal Rate of Return) function calculates the internal rate of return for a series of cash flows. To use IRR, type =IRR(cashflow_range, [guess]). For example, to calculate the IRR for a series of cash flows in cells A1 to A5, type =IRR(A1:A5) and press Enter. The result will display the internal rate of return.

Step 2: Using the NPV Function. The NPV (Net Present Value) function calculates the net present value of an investment based on a series of periodic cash flows and a discount rate. To use NPV, type =NPV(rate, value_range). For example, to calculate the NPV of an investment with a discount rate of 8% and cash flows in cells A1 to A5, type =NPV(8%, A1:A5) and press Enter. The result will display the net present value.

Step 3: Using the XIRR Function. The XIRR function calculates the internal rate of return for a schedule of cash flows that are not necessarily periodic. To use XIRR, type =XIRR(cashflow_range, date_range). For example, to calculate the XIRR for cash flows in cells A1 to A5 with corresponding dates in cells B1 to B5, type =XIRR(A1:A5, B1:B5) and press Enter. The result will display the internal rate of return.

Step 4: Using the XNPV Function. The XNPV function calculates the net present value for a schedule of cash flows that are not necessarily periodic. To use XNPV, type =XNPV(rate, cashflow_range, date_range). For example, to calculate the XNPV of an investment with a discount rate of 6%, cash flows in cells A1 to A5, and corresponding dates in cells B1 to B5, type =XNPV(6%, A1:A5, B1:B5) and press Enter. The result will display the net present value.

Practical Examples

Example 1: Calculating Loan Payments. Suppose you are considering a loan of $150,000 with an annual interest rate of 5% and a term of 15 years. To calculate the monthly payment, use the PMT function: =PMT(5%/12, 15*12, -150000). This will display the monthly payment amount.

Example 2: Determining Future Value of Savings. Suppose you save $200 per month with an annual interest rate of 4% for 10 years. To calculate the future value of these savings, use the FV function: =FV(4%/12, 10*12, -200). This will display the future value of your savings.

Example 3: Finding Present Value of an Investment. Suppose you expect to receive $1,000 per month for the next 5 years and want to know the present value of this investment with an annual interest rate of 3%. Use the PV function: =PV(3%/12, 5*12, -1000). This will display the present value of the investment.

Example 4: Calculating Internal Rate of Return. Suppose you have a series of cash flows: -$1,000, $300, $400, $500, and $600. To calculate the IRR for these cash flows, use the IRR function: =IRR(A1:A5). This will display the internal rate of return.

Example 5: Computing Net Present Value. Suppose you have an investment with cash flows of -$1,000, $200, $300, $400, and $500, and a discount rate of 7%. To calculate the NPV, use the NPV function: =NPV(7%, A1:A5). This will display the net present value.

Statistical Functions

Google Sheets offers a comprehensive set of statistical functions that allow you to perform various statistical analyses, from basic descriptive statistics to more complex inferential statistics. These functions are essential for data analysis, research, and decision-making.

Basic Statistical Functions

Step 1: Using the AVERAGE Function. The AVERAGE function calculates the mean of a range of cells. To use it, click on the cell where you want the result, type =AVERAGE(followed by the range of cells. For example, =AVERAGE(A1:A10) calculates the average of values in A1 to A10.

Step 2: Using the MEDIAN Function. The MEDIAN function returns the median of a range of cells. Click on the cell where you want the result, type =MEDIAN(followed by the range of cells. For example, =MEDIAN(A1:A10) calculates the median of values in A1 to A10.

Step 3: Using the MODE Function. The MODE function returns the most frequently occurring value in a range of cells. To use it, type =MODE(followed by the range of cells. For example, =MODE(A1:A10) returns the mode of values in A1 to A10.

Step 4: Using the MIN and MAX Functions. The MIN function returns the smallest value in a range, while the MAX function returns the largest. To use these functions, type =MIN(A1:A10) or =MAX(A1:A10) and press Enter. The result will display the smallest or largest value in the specified range.

Step 5: Using the COUNT and COUNTA Functions. The COUNT function counts the number of cells that contain numbers in a range, while the COUNTA function counts all non-empty cells. Type =COUNT(followed by the range of cells. For example, =COUNT(A1:A10) counts the number of cells in A1 to A10 that contain numbers. Use =COUNTA(A1:A10) to count all non-empty cells in the range.

Advanced Statistical Functions

Step 1: Using the STDEV Function. The STDEV function calculates the standard deviation of a range of cells, measuring the amount of variation or dispersion in a dataset. To use STDEV, type =STDEV(followed by the range of cells. For example, =STDEV(A1:A10) calculates the standard deviation of values in A1 to A10.

Step 2: Using the VAR Function. The VAR function calculates the variance of a range of cells, indicating how much the values differ from the mean. To use VAR, type =VAR(followed by the range of cells. For example, =VAR(A1:A10) calculates the variance of values in A1 to A10.

Step 3: Using the CORREL Function. The CORREL function calculates the correlation coefficient between two datasets, showing the strength and direction of the relationship. To use CORREL, type =CORREL(data_y, data_x). For example, =CORREL(A1:A10, B1:B10) calculates the correlation between the values in A1 to A10 and B1 to B10.

Step 4: Using the FORECAST Function. The FORECAST function predicts a future value based on existing values using linear regression. To use FORECAST, type =FORECAST(x, data_y, data_x). For example, =FORECAST(C1, B1:B10, A1:A10) predicts the value at x = C1 based on the linear regression of values in A1 to A10 and B1 to B10.

Step 5: Using the LINEST Function. The LINEST function calculates the statistics for a line by performing a linear regression. To use LINEST, type =LINEST(data_y, data_x, [const], [stats]). For example, =LINEST(B1:B10, A1:A10, TRUE, TRUE) returns the statistics for the linear regression of values in A1 to A10 and B1 to B10.

Practical Examples

Example 1: Calculating Basic Descriptive Statistics. Suppose you have a dataset in column A and you want to calculate the mean, median, mode, minimum, maximum, count, and standard deviation. Use the following functions:

- Mean: =AVERAGE(A1:A10)
- Median: =MEDIAN(A1:A10)
- Mode: =MODE(A1:A10)
- Minimum: =MIN(A1:A10)
- Maximum: =MAX(A1:A10)
- Count: =COUNT(A1:A10)
- Standard Deviation: =STDEV(A1:A10)

Example 2: Analyzing Variance and Correlation. Suppose you have two datasets in columns A and B and you want to calculate the variance and correlation. Use the following functions:

- Variance: =VAR(A1:A10)
- Correlation: =CORREL(A1:A10, B1:B10)

Example 3: Forecasting Future Values. Suppose you have sales data in column A and corresponding time periods in column B, and you want to forecast future sales. Use the FORECAST function: =FORECAST(C1, A1:A10, B1:B10). This will predict the sales value at the time period specified in cell C1.

Example 4: Performing Linear Regression Analysis. Suppose you have a dependent variable in column A and an independent variable in column B, and you want to perform a linear regression analysis. Use the LINEST function: =LINEST(A1:A10, B1:B10, TRUE, TRUE). This will return the statistics for the linear regression.

Text Functions

Google Sheets provides a robust set of text functions that allow you to manipulate and transform text strings within your spreadsheets. These functions are essential for cleaning up data, formatting text, and creating dynamic text-based formulas.

Basic Text Functions

Step 1: Using the CONCATENATE Function. The CONCATENATE function combines multiple text strings into one. To use CONCATENATE, type =CONCATENATE(followed by the text strings or cell references you want to combine. For example, to combine the text in cells A1 and B1 with a space between them, type =CONCATENATE(A1, " ", B1) and press Enter. The result will display the combined text.

Step 2: Using the SPLIT Function. The SPLIT function divides a text string into separate parts based on a specified delimiter. To use SPLIT, type =SPLIT(followed by the text string or cell reference and the delimiter. For example, to split the text in cell A1 into separate parts based on spaces, type =SPLIT(A1, " ") and press Enter. The result will display the split text in multiple cells.

Step 3: Using the JOIN Function. The JOIN function combines multiple text strings into one, separated by a specified delimiter. To use JOIN, type =JOIN(delimiter, range). For example, to join the text in cells A1 to A3 with commas, type =JOIN(", ", A1:A3) and press Enter. The result will display the combined text with commas separating the original text strings.

Step 4: Using the LEFT, RIGHT, and MID Functions. These functions extract specific parts of a text string.

- LEFT: Returns the leftmost characters from a text string. Use =LEFT(text, number_of_characters). For example, =LEFT(A1, 3) returns the first three characters of the text in cell A1.
- RIGHT: Returns the rightmost characters from a text string. Use =RIGHT(text, number_of_characters). For example, =RIGHT(A1, 3) returns the last three characters of the text in cell A1.
- MID: Returns characters from the middle of a text string. Use =MID(text, start, number_of_characters). For example, =MID(A1, 2, 3) returns three characters starting from the second character of the text in cell A1.

Advanced Text Functions

Step 1: Using the LEN Function. The LEN function returns the length of a text string. To use LEN, type =LEN(text). For example, =LEN(A1) returns the number of characters in the text in cell A1.

Step 2: Using the FIND and SEARCH Functions. These functions locate the position of a substring within a text string.

- FIND: Case-sensitive. Use =FIND(search_for, text_to_search, [starting_at]). For example, =FIND("abc", A1) returns the position of "abc" in cell A1.
- SEARCH: Case-insensitive. Use =SEARCH(search_for, text_to_search, [starting_at]). For example, =SEARCH("abc", A1) returns the position of "abc" in cell A1 regardless of case.

Step 3: Using the SUBSTITUTE Function. The SUBSTITUTE function replaces occurrences of a specified text string within another text string. To use SUBSTITUTE, type =SUBSTITUTE(text, old_text, new_text, [instance_num]). For example, =SUBSTITUTE(A1, "old", "new") replaces all instances of "old" with "new" in the text in cell A1.

Step 4: Using the REPT Function. The REPT function repeats a text string a specified number of times. To use REPT, type =REPT(text, number_of_times). For example, =REPT("abc", 3) repeats "abc" three times.

Step 5: Using the TEXT Function. The TEXT function formats a number and converts it to text. To use TEXT, type =TEXT(number, format). For example, =TEXT(1234.567, "$#,##0.00") formats the number as currency.

Practical Examples

Example 1: Combining Names. Suppose you have first names in column A and last names in column B, and you want to combine them into full names in column C. Use the CONCATENATE function: =CONCATENATE(A1, " ", B1). This will display the full names in column C.

Example 2: Extracting Initials. Suppose you have full names in column A and you want to extract the initials. Use the LEFT and FIND functions together: =LEFT(A1, 1) & "." & MID(A1, FIND(" ", A1) + 1, 1) & ".". This will display the initials in column B.

Example 3: Formatting Phone Numbers. Suppose you have phone numbers in column A and you want to format them as (123) 456-7890. Use the TEXT function: =TEXT(A1, "(###) ###-####"). This will display the formatted phone numbers in column B.

Example 4: Removing Extra Spaces. Suppose you have text with extra spaces in column A and you want to clean it up. Use the TRIM function: =TRIM(A1). This will remove the extra spaces and display the cleaned text in column B.

Example 5: Replacing Text. Suppose you have a list of products in column A and you want to replace "Old Product" with "New Product." Use the SUBSTITUTE function: =SUBSTITUTE(A1, "Old Product", "New Product"). This will display the updated product names in column B.

Google Sheets provides a set of info functions that offer valuable information about your data, your spreadsheet, and the environment in which you are working. These functions are useful for debugging, data validation, and understanding your data better.

Basic Info Functions

Step 1: Using the ISNUMBER Function. The ISNUMBER function checks whether a value is a number. To use ISNUMBER, type =ISNUMBER(value). For example, =ISNUMBER(A1) returns TRUE if the value in cell A1 is a number, and FALSE otherwise.

Step 2: Using the ISBLANK Function. The ISBLANK function checks whether a cell is empty. To use ISBLANK, type =ISBLANK(value). For example, =ISBLANK(A1) returns TRUE if cell A1 is empty, and FALSE otherwise.

Step 3: Using the ISTEXT Function. The ISTEXT function checks whether a value is text. To use ISTEXT, type =ISTEXT(value). For example, =ISTEXT(A1) returns TRUE if the value in cell A1 is text, and FALSE otherwise.

Step 4: Using the ISNONTEXT Function. The ISNONTEXT function checks whether a value is not text. To use ISNONTEXT, type =ISNONTEXT(value). For example, =ISNONTEXT(A1) returns TRUE if the value in cell A1 is not text, and FALSE otherwise.

Step 5: Using the ISERROR and ISERR Functions. These functions check whether a value is an error. ISERROR returns TRUE for any error, while ISERR excludes the #N/A error.

- To use ISERROR, type =ISERROR(value). For example, =ISERROR(A1) returns TRUE if there is any error in cell A1.
- To use ISERR, type =ISERR(value). For example, =ISERR(A1) returns TRUE if there is any error in cell A1 except #N/A.

Step 6: Using the ISNA Function. The ISNA function checks whether a value is the #N/A error. To use ISNA, type =ISNA(value). For example, =ISNA(A1) returns TRUE if cell A1 contains the #N/A error, and FALSE otherwise.

Step 7: Using the TYPE Function. The TYPE function returns a number representing the type of value in a cell. To use TYPE, type =TYPE(value). For example, =TYPE(A1) returns:

- 1 for numbers
- 2 for text
- 4 for logical values
- 16 for errors

- 64 for array

Advanced Info Functions

Step 1: Using the CELL Function. The CELL function returns information about the formatting, location, or contents of a cell. To use CELL, type =CELL(info_type, [reference]). For example, =CELL("address", A1) returns the address of cell A1.

Step 2: Using the INFO Function. The INFO function returns information about the current operating environment. To use INFO, type =INFO(info_type). For example, =INFO("directory") returns the current directory or folder.

Step 3: Using the ERROR.TYPE Function. The ERROR.TYPE function returns a number corresponding to a specific error value. To use ERROR.TYPE, type =ERROR.TYPE(error_val). For example, =ERROR.TYPE(A1) returns:

- 1 for #NULL!
- 2 for #DIV/0!
- 3 for #VALUE!
- 4 for #REF!
- 5 for #NAME?
- 6 for #NUM!
- 7 for #N/A
- 8 for all other errors

Practical Examples

Example 1: Validating Numeric Data. Suppose you have data in column A and you want to check if each value is a number. Use the ISNUMBER function: =ISNUMBER(A1). This will return TRUE for numeric values and FALSE for non-numeric values.

Example 2: Identifying Blank Cells. Suppose you have data in column A and you want to identify empty cells. Use the ISBLANK function: =ISBLANK(A1). This will return TRUE for empty cells and FALSE for non-empty cells.

Example 3: Error Checking. Suppose you have formulas in column A and you want to check for errors. Use the ISERROR function: =ISERROR(A1). This will return TRUE for any errors and FALSE for non-errors. To exclude #N/A errors, use the ISERR function: =ISERR(A1).

Example 4: Extracting Cell Information. Suppose you want to get the address of a specific cell. Use the CELL function: =CELL("address", A1). This will return the address of cell A1. To get the column number of a cell, use =CELL("col", A1).

Example 5: Checking Data Types. Suppose you have mixed data in column A and you want to identify the type of each value. Use the TYPE function: =TYPE(A1). This will return a number representing the type of value in cell A1 (e.g., 1 for numbers, 2 for text).

Example 6: Environment Information. Suppose you need information about your current directory. Use the INFO function: =INFO("directory"). This will return the current directory or folder.

Lookup Functions

Lookup functions in Google Sheets are essential tools for searching and retrieving specific data from a large dataset. These functions can help you find and extract information based on criteria, making them invaluable for data analysis, reporting, and decision-making.

Using the VLOOKUP Function

The VLOOKUP function searches for a value in the first column of a range and returns a value in the same row from a specified column.

Step 1: Basic Usage. To use VLOOKUP, type =VLOOKUP(search_key, range, index, [is_sorted]). For example, to search for a product name in column A and return its price from column B, type =VLOOKUP("ProductA", A1:B10, 2, FALSE) and press Enter. This will return the price of "ProductA."

Step 2: Exact Match. To ensure an exact match, set the is_sorted parameter to FALSE. For example, =VLOOKUP("ProductA", A1:B10, 2, FALSE) will search for an exact match of "ProductA."

Step 3: Approximate Match. To allow an approximate match, set the is_sorted parameter to TRUE or omit it. For example, =VLOOKUP("ProductA", A1:B10, 2, TRUE) will return the closest match to "ProductA."

Using the HLOOKUP Function

The HLOOKUP function searches for a value in the first row of a range and returns a value in the same column from a specified row.

Step 1: Basic Usage. To use HLOOKUP, type =HLOOKUP(search_key, range, index, [is_sorted]). For example, to search for a month in the first row and return its sales from the second row, type =HLOOKUP("January", A1:D2, 2, FALSE) and press Enter. This will return the sales for "January."

Step 2: Exact Match. To ensure an exact match, set the is_sorted parameter to FALSE. For example, =HLOOKUP("January", A1:D2, 2, FALSE) will search for an exact match of "January."

Step 3: Approximate Match. To allow an approximate match, set the is_sorted parameter to TRUE or omit it. For example, =HLOOKUP("January", A1:D2, 2, TRUE) will return the closest match to "January."

Using the INDEX and MATCH Functions

The INDEX and MATCH functions are often used together to perform more flexible lookups than VLOOKUP or HLOOKUP.

Step 1: Using the MATCH Function. The MATCH function searches for a value in a range and returns its relative position. To use MATCH, type =MATCH(search_key, range, [match_type]). For example, =MATCH("ProductA", A1:A10, 0) returns the position of "ProductA" in the range A1

.

Step 2: Using the INDEX Function. The INDEX function returns the value of a cell in a specified row and column. To use INDEX, type =INDEX(range, row_num, [column_num]). For example, =INDEX(A1:B10, 2, 2) returns the value in the second row and second column of the range A1

.

Step 3: Combining INDEX and MATCH. To perform a lookup with INDEX and MATCH, use MATCH to find the row number and INDEX to return the value. For example, to find the price of "ProductA" in column B, type =INDEX(B1:B10, MATCH("ProductA", A1:A10, 0)). This will return the price of "ProductA."

Using the LOOKUP Function

The LOOKUP function searches for a value in a range and returns a value from the same position in a second range.

Step 1: Basic Usage. To use LOOKUP, type =LOOKUP(search_key, search_range, result_range). For example, to search for a product name in column A and return its price from column B, type =LOOKUP("ProductA", A1:A10, B1:B10) and press Enter. This will return the price of "ProductA."

Step 2: Handling Missing Values. If the search value is not found, LOOKUP returns the largest value in the search range that is less than or equal to the search key. For example, if "ProductA" is not found, LOOKUP will return the next closest match.

Practical Examples

Example 1: Using VLOOKUP for Inventory Management. Suppose you have a list of products in column A and their prices in column B, and you want to find the price of a specific product. Use the VLOOKUP function: =VLOOKUP("ProductA", A1:B10, 2, FALSE). This will display the price of "ProductA."

Example 2: Using HLOOKUP for Monthly Sales Data. Suppose you have sales data for each month in the first row and want to find the sales for "January." Use the HLOOKUP function: =HLOOKUP("January", A1:D2, 2, FALSE). This will display the sales for "January."

Example 3: Combining INDEX and MATCH for Flexible Lookups. Suppose you have a list of employees in column A and their departments in column B, and you want to find the department of a specific employee. Use INDEX and MATCH: =INDEX(B1:B10, MATCH("EmployeeA", A1:A10, 0)). This will display the department of "EmployeeA."

Example 4: Using LOOKUP for Grade Conversion. Suppose you have a list of scores in column A and corresponding grades in column B, and you want to find the grade for a specific score. Use the LOOKUP function: =LOOKUP(85, A1:A10, B1:B10). This will display the grade for the score 85.

Web Functions

Google Sheets includes several web functions that allow you to interact with online data directly from your spreadsheet. These functions are useful for importing data from the web, connecting to APIs, and retrieving real-time information.

Using the IMPORTHTML Function

The IMPORTHTML function imports data from a table or list within an HTML page.

Step 1: Basic Usage. To use IMPORTHTML, type =IMPORTHTML(url, query, index). For example, to import the first table from a Wikipedia page, type =IMPORTHTML("https://en.wikipedia.org/wiki/List_of_countries_by_population_(United_Nations)", "table", 1) and press Enter. This will import the first table from the specified URL into your spreadsheet.

Step 2: Importing Lists. You can also import lists using IMPORTHTML. For example, to import the first list from the same Wikipedia page, type =IMPORTHTML("https://en.wikipedia.org/wiki/List_of_countries_by_population_(United_Nations)", "list", 1) and press Enter. This will import the first list from the specified URL.

Using the IMPORTXML Function

The IMPORTXML function imports data from an XML, HTML, CSV, TSV, or RSS/Atom feed.

Step 1: Basic Usage. To use IMPORTXML, type =IMPORTXML(url, xpath_query). For example, to import the title of the Wikipedia page on Google, type =IMPORTXML("https://en.wikipedia.org/wiki/Google", "//title") and press Enter. This will import the title of the specified page.

Step 2: Extracting Specific Data. You can use XPath queries to extract specific data from the web page. For example, to extract all the hyperlinks from the Google Wikipedia page, type =IMPORTXML("https://en.wikipedia.org/wiki/Google", "//a/@href") and press Enter. This will import all the hyperlinks from the specified page.

Using the IMPORTDATA Function

The IMPORTDATA function imports data from a CSV or TSV file.

Step 1: Basic Usage. To use IMPORTDATA, type =IMPORTDATA(url). For example, to import data from a public CSV file, type =IMPORTDATA("http://example.com/data.csv") and press Enter. This will import the data from the specified URL into your spreadsheet.

Step 2: Handling Large Datasets. When importing large datasets, ensure that the file size is manageable within the limits of Google Sheets. If the dataset is too large, consider breaking it into smaller parts or using another method to handle the data.

Using the IMPORTFEED Function

The IMPORTFEED function imports an RSS or Atom feed.

Step 1: Basic Usage. To use IMPORTFEED, type =IMPORTFEED(url, [query], [headers], [num_items]). For example, to import the latest headlines from a news RSS feed, type =IMPORTFEED("https://rss.cnn.com/rss/edition.rss") and press Enter. This will import the latest headlines from the specified RSS feed.

Step 2: Customizing the Query. You can customize the query to fetch specific data from the feed. For example, to import the titles and links from the feed, type =IMPORTFEED("https://rss.cnn.com/rss/edition.rss", "items title, link") and press Enter. This will import the titles and links from the specified feed.

Using the IMPORTRANGE Function

The IMPORTRANGE function imports a range of cells from a specified spreadsheet.

Step 1: Basic Usage. To use IMPORTRANGE, type =IMPORTRANGE(spreadsheet_url, range_string). For example, to import data from the range A1

in another Google Sheets document, type =IMPORTRANGE("https://docs.google.com/spreadsheets/d/your-spreadsheet-id/edit", "Sheet1!A1:B10") and press Enter. This will import the specified range from the specified spreadsheet.

Step 2: Granting Access. The first time you use IMPORTRANGE, you will need to grant access to the source spreadsheet. Click "Allow access" when prompted to enable the function to pull data from the specified spreadsheet.

Practical Examples

Example 1: Importing Stock Prices. Suppose you want to import real-time stock prices from a financial website. Use the IMPORTXML function: =IMPORTXML("https://finance.yahoo.com/quote/GOOGL", "//span[@class='Trsdu(0.3s) Fw(b) Fz(36px) Mb(-4px) D(ib)']"). This will import the current stock price of Google from Yahoo Finance.

Example 2: Importing Weather Data. Suppose you want to import weather data from a weather website. Use the IMPORTXML function: =IMPORTXML("https://weather.com/weather/today/l/USCA1116:1:US", "//span[@class='CurrentConditions--tempValue--3KcTQ']"). This will import the current temperature for a specified location.

Example 3: Importing Data from Another Spreadsheet. Suppose you have a master spreadsheet with all your sales data and want to import a specific range into a new spreadsheet for analysis. Use the IMPORTRANGE function: =IMPORTRANGE("https://docs.google.com/spreadsheets/d/your-spreadsheet-id/edit", "SalesData!A1:D10"). This will import the specified range from the master spreadsheet.

Example 4: Importing News Headlines. Suppose you want to keep track of the latest news headlines. Use the IMPORTFEED function: =IMPORTFEED("https://rss.nytimes.com/services/xml/rss/nyt/HomePage.xml"). This will import the latest headlines from The New York Times RSS feed.

Example 5: Importing Sports Scores. Suppose you want to track sports scores from a sports website. Use the IMPORTXML function: =IMPORTXML("https://www.espn.com/nba/scoreboard", "//div[@class='score-container']"). This will import the latest sports scores from ESPN.

Google Slide

Google Slides is a versatile, cloud-based presentation tool that allows you to create, edit, and collaborate on presentations online. It is part of the Google Workspace suite and provides a wide range of features to enhance your presentations.

Getting Started with Google Slides

Step 1: Access Google Slides. To begin, visit slides.google.com in your web browser or open the Google Slides app on your mobile device. Sign in with your Google Workspace or personal Google account.

Step 2: Create a new presentation. On the Google Slides homepage, click on the "+" (plus) icon labeled "Blank" to create a new presentation. You can also choose a template from the template gallery to start with a pre-designed layout.

Step 3: Name your presentation. Click on the "Untitled presentation" field at the top left of the page and type in your desired title. This will help you easily identify your presentation in Google Drive later.

Adding and Managing Slides

Step 1: Add new slides. To add a new slide, click on the "+" icon in the toolbar or right-click in the slide pane on the left and select "New slide." You can also use the keyboard shortcut Ctrl + M (Cmd + M on Mac) to add a new slide.

Step 2: Choose slide layouts. Google Slides offers various slide layouts to suit different content types. Click on the "Layout" dropdown menu in the toolbar to choose a layout for your slide, such as title slide, section header, two columns, or a blank slide.

Step 3: Organize your slides. Rearrange the order of your slides by dragging them up or down in the slide pane on the left. You can also right-click on a slide to duplicate, delete, or skip it.

Adding Content to Slides

Step 1: Add text. Click on a text box or double-click on an empty area of the slide to add text. Use the formatting toolbar at the top to change the font, size, color, alignment, and other text properties.

You can also add additional text boxes by clicking "Insert" > "Text box" and clicking on the slide where you want the text box to appear.

Step 2: Insert images. To add images, click on "Insert" > "Image" and choose an option: upload from your computer, search the web, or select from your Google Drive or Photos. Drag the image to reposition it and use the handles to resize it.

Step 3: Add shapes and lines. Click on "Insert" > "Shape" to add shapes such as rectangles, circles, arrows, and more. Click on "Insert" > "Line" to draw lines or connectors. Use the formatting options in the toolbar to change the color, border, and other properties of the shapes and lines.

Step 4: Embed videos. To add a video, click on "Insert" > "Video" and choose to either search YouTube, paste a URL, or select from your Google Drive. Position and resize the video as needed on the slide.

Step 5: Add charts and tables. To insert a chart, click on "Insert" > "Chart" and choose the type of chart (bar, column, line, pie, etc.). To insert a table, click on "Insert" > "Table" and select the number of rows and columns. Customize the appearance and data of charts and tables using the options in the toolbar and the "Chart editor" or "Table properties."

Collaborating on Presentations

Step 1: Share your presentation. Click the "Share" button in the top right corner to invite others to view or edit your presentation. Enter the email addresses of the people you want to share with and set their permissions (Viewer, Commenter, or Editor). Click "Send" to share the presentation.

Step 2: Collaborate in real-time. Multiple people can work on the presentation simultaneously. Each collaborator's cursor is highlighted in a different color, and you can see their changes in real-time. Use the chat feature by clicking on the chat icon in the top right corner to communicate with collaborators without leaving the presentation.

Step 3: Comment and suggest edits. Highlight text or select an object, then click the comment icon or right-click and select "Comment" to leave feedback. Collaborators can reply to comments and resolve them once addressed. Use "Suggesting" mode to propose changes without altering the original content. To switch to suggesting mode, click on the pencil icon in the top right corner and select "Suggesting."

Customizing Your Presentation

Step 1: Apply themes. Google Slides offers various themes to give your presentation a cohesive look. Click on "Theme" in the toolbar and choose from the available themes. You can also customize the theme colors and fonts by clicking "Customize" at the bottom of the theme sidebar.

Step 2: Use transitions and animations. To add transitions between slides, click on "Slide" > "Change transition" and choose a transition type from the sidebar. To animate objects on a slide, select the object, click on "Insert" > "Animation," and choose an animation effect. Adjust the animation settings in the sidebar to control the timing and order of animations.

Step 3: Customize the slide master. The slide master allows you to make global changes to the appearance of your slides. Click on "Slide" > "Edit master" to open the slide master view. Here, you can customize the layout, background, and styles for all slides in your presentation.

Presenting Your Slides

Step 1: Present your slides. To start presenting, click on the "Present" button in the top right corner or press Ctrl + F5 (Cmd + Shift + Enter on Mac). Use the arrow keys or click the on-screen arrows to navigate through your slides.

Step 2: Use presenter view. Presenter view provides tools to help you present more effectively, including a timer, speaker notes, and a preview of the next slide. To enable presenter view, click on the arrow next to the "Present" button and select "Presenter view."

Step 3: Share your presentation. You can share your presentation with a broader audience by publishing it to the web. Click on "File" > "Publish to the web," choose your publishing settings, and click "Publish." Copy the provided link and share it with your audience.

Google Forms

Google Forms is a versatile tool that allows you to create surveys, quizzes, and forms to collect data efficiently. It is part of the Google Workspace suite and offers a wide range of features to customize your forms and analyze responses.

Getting Started with Google Forms

Step 1: Access Google Forms. To begin, visit forms.google.com in your web browser or open the Google Forms app on your mobile device. Sign in with your Google Workspace or personal Google account.

Step 2: Create a new form. On the Google Forms homepage, click on the "+" (plus) icon labeled "Blank" to create a new form. You can also choose a template from the template gallery to start with a pre-designed layout.

Step 3: Name your form. Click on the "Untitled form" field at the top left of the page and type in your desired title. This will help you easily identify your form in Google Drive later. You can also add a description below the title to provide additional information about the form's purpose.

Adding and Managing Questions

Step 1: Add questions. Click on the "+" icon in the toolbar on the right to add a new question. You can choose from various question types, including multiple choice, short answer, paragraph, checkboxes, dropdown, linear scale, and more. Select the appropriate question type based on the information you want to collect.

Step 2: Customize question settings. For each question, you can add the question text, options (if applicable), and any additional instructions. Use the toggle switch at the bottom right of the question to make it a required question, ensuring respondents cannot skip it.

Step 3: Organize your questions. Rearrange the order of your questions by clicking and dragging them up or down. You can also use the "Duplicate" icon to create a copy of a question or the "Trash" icon to delete a question.

Step 4: Add sections. To group related questions, click on the "Add section" icon in the toolbar. This will divide your form into different sections, allowing respondents to navigate through the form more easily. You can add titles and descriptions to each section to provide context.

Customizing Your Form

Step 1: Change the theme. Click on the "Palette" icon in the toolbar to customize the appearance of your form. You can choose from various theme colors, add a background image, and change the font style. This helps make your form visually appealing and aligned with your brand or project.

Step 2: Add images and videos. To enhance your form with visual content, click on the "Image" or "Video" icon in the toolbar. You can upload images from your computer, search the web, or select from your Google Drive. For videos, you can paste a YouTube URL or search for a video directly within Google Forms.

Step 3: Use logic branching. Logic branching allows you to direct respondents to different sections of the form based on their answers. To set up logic branching, click on the three-dot menu icon on a question and select "Go to section based on answer." Specify which section respondents should be directed to based on their chosen answer.

Collecting Responses

Step 1: Configure response settings. Click on the "Settings" icon in the top right corner to configure response settings. You can choose to collect email addresses, limit responses to one per person, and allow respondents to edit their responses after submission. You can also set a confirmation message that respondents will see after submitting the form.

Step 2: Share your form. Click on the "Send" button in the top right corner to share your form with others. You can send the form via email, share a link, or embed it on a website. Use the sharing options to control who can access and respond to the form.

Step 3: View responses. As responses come in, you can view them by clicking on the "Responses" tab at the top of the form. Here, you can see a summary of responses, individual responses, and responses in a spreadsheet format. Click on the green Sheets icon to open the responses in Google Sheets for further analysis.

Step 4: Analyze responses. Use the summary and individual response views to analyze the collected data. Google Forms automatically generates charts and graphs for quantitative data, making it easy to visualize and interpret the results. For more advanced analysis, use Google Sheets to apply filters, create pivot tables, and perform statistical calculations.

Using Google Forms for Quizzes

Step 1: Create a quiz. To create a quiz, click on the "Settings" icon, go to the "Quizzes" tab, and toggle the switch to make this a quiz. You can assign point values to each question, set correct answers, and provide feedback for correct and incorrect answers.

Step 2: Customize quiz settings. In the quiz settings, you can choose to release grades immediately after submission or later after manual review. You can also decide what respondents can see after submitting the quiz, such as missed questions, correct answers, and point values.

Step 3: Grade responses. Once responses are submitted, you can grade them by clicking on the "Responses" tab and selecting the "Individual" view. Here, you can review each respondent's answers, assign points, and provide feedback. If you chose to release grades later, you can manually send the grades to respondents once grading is complete.

Data Collection and Analysis

Google Forms is not just a tool for creating surveys and quizzes; it is also a powerful platform for collecting and analyzing data. With its integration into Google Sheets, you can easily manage responses, perform data analysis, and generate insights.

Setting Up Data Collection

Step 1: Create and Customize Your Form. Begin by creating a form in Google Forms, as described in the previous section. Customize your form with various question types to collect the specific data you need. Use text boxes for open-ended questions, multiple-choice or checkboxes for predefined options, and scales or grids for rating or comparison questions.

Step 2: Configure Response Settings. Click on the "Settings" icon in the top right corner to configure how you want to collect and manage responses. You can:

- **Collect email addresses**: Ensure you can contact respondents later.
- **Limit responses to one per person**: Prevent duplicate entries.
- **Allow respondents to edit responses**: Enable respondents to update their answers if needed.
- **Show progress bar**: Help respondents understand how much of the form is left.

Step 3: Share Your Form. Click on the "Send" button to share your form. You can send it via email, share a link, or embed it on a website. Use these options to reach your target audience effectively.

Managing Responses

Step 1: View Responses. Once your form is live and respondents start submitting their answers, click on the "Responses" tab at the top of the form to view the collected data. Here, you can see a summary of all responses, individual responses, and detailed data in a spreadsheet format.

Step 2: Use Google Sheets. For more advanced data management and analysis, click on the green Sheets icon in the "Responses" tab. This will create a Google Sheets document linked to your form, where all responses are automatically recorded. In Google Sheets, you can:

- **Sort and filter data**: Organize your data by different criteria to find specific information.
- **Use formulas and functions**: Perform calculations, summarize data, and analyze trends using Google Sheets' built-in functions.
- **Create charts and graphs**: Visualize your data with various chart types to make insights more accessible.

Analyzing Data

Step 1: Summary of Responses. Google Forms provides a summary view that includes automatically generated charts and graphs for quantitative data. This quick overview helps you identify patterns and trends at a glance.

Step 2: Detailed Analysis in Google Sheets. For deeper analysis, use Google Sheets:

- **Pivot Tables**: Create pivot tables to summarize large datasets and explore different dimensions of your data.
- **Statistical Functions**: Apply statistical functions like AVERAGE, MEDIAN, STDEV, and CORREL to understand the distribution and relationships within your data.
- **Conditional Formatting**: Highlight important data points or anomalies with conditional formatting rules.

Step 3: Filtering and Sorting Data. In Google Sheets, use the filter and sort options to manage your data more effectively:

- **Filter**: Create filters to view subsets of your data based on specific criteria.
- **Sort**: Arrange your data in ascending or descending order based on one or more columns.

Step 4: Creating Visualizations. Visualize your data to make it easier to interpret:

- **Charts**: Use bar charts, pie charts, line graphs, and more to represent your data visually.

- **Custom Dashboards**: Create custom dashboards that compile multiple visualizations and key metrics in one place.

Using Data for Decision-Making

Step 1: Identify Key Insights. Analyze the summarized data and visualizations to identify key insights and trends. Look for patterns that can inform your decisions.

Step 2: Share Findings. Use Google Sheets' sharing features to collaborate with team members. You can share the entire sheet or specific charts and tables. Use the "Comment" and "Notes" features to discuss specific data points and insights.

Step 3: Apply Insights. Use the insights gained from your data to make informed decisions. Whether you're using Google Forms for customer feedback, employee surveys, market research, or educational assessments, the data collected can guide your next steps.

Step 4: Automate Data Analysis with Add-ons. Explore Google Sheets add-ons like "AutoCrat" for document merging, "FormMule" for email notification workflows, and "Supermetrics" for advanced data integration. These tools can automate parts of your data collection and analysis process, making it more efficient.

Practical Examples

Example 1: Customer Satisfaction Survey. Suppose you conduct a customer satisfaction survey to collect feedback on your products. Use Google Forms to design the survey, collect responses, and link the data to Google Sheets. Analyze the data to find satisfaction trends, identify common issues, and determine areas for improvement.

Example 2: Employee Feedback Form. Create an employee feedback form to gather opinions on workplace environment and management. Use the response summary to quickly gauge overall sentiment and use Google Sheets to analyze detailed feedback, track changes over time, and identify specific areas that need attention.

Example 3: Market Research Questionnaire. Design a market research questionnaire to understand customer preferences and market trends. Share the form with your target audience, collect the data, and analyze the responses in Google Sheets. Use pivot tables and charts to identify key market segments and preferences.

Example 4: Educational Assessment. Create a quiz or assessment for students using Google Forms. Collect their responses and use the quiz feature to automatically grade the answers. Analyze the results to identify common learning gaps and adjust your teaching strategies accordingly.

Google Translate

Google Translate is a powerful tool that enables you to translate text, speech, images, and websites between multiple languages. Whether you're traveling, studying, or working in a multilingual environment, Google Translate can help you communicate and understand information across language barriers.

Using Google Translate for Text Translation

Step 1: Access Google Translate. Visit translate.google.com in your web browser or download the Google Translate app on your mobile device from the Google Play Store or Apple App Store.

Step 2: Select languages. Choose the source language (the language of the text you want to translate) and the target language (the language you want to translate the text into). You can do this by clicking on the language dropdown menus at the top of the page.

Step 3: Enter text. Type or paste the text you want to translate into the left text box. The translation will appear automatically in the right text box.

Step 4: Copy or share the translation. You can copy the translated text by clicking on the copy icon or share it directly using the share icon. If you're using the mobile app, you can also share the translation via other apps on your device.

Step 5: Listen to the pronunciation. Click on the speaker icon next to the translated text to hear its pronunciation. This feature is especially useful for learning how to pronounce words and phrases correctly.

Translating Speech

Step 1: Open the Google Translate app. Open the app on your mobile device.

Step 2: Select languages. Choose the source and target languages as described above.

Step 3: Tap the microphone icon. Tap the microphone icon to activate speech translation mode.

Step 4: Speak into your device. Speak clearly into your device's microphone. Google Translate will transcribe and translate your speech in real-time, displaying the translation on the screen.

Step 5: Listen to the translation. Tap the speaker icon next to the translated text to hear it spoken aloud.

Translating Images

Step 1: Open the Google Translate app. Open the app on your mobile device.

Step 2: Select languages. Choose the source and target languages.

Step 3: Tap the camera icon. Tap the camera icon to activate the image translation mode.

Step 4: Point your camera at the text. Point your device's camera at the text you want to translate. Google Translate will detect and translate the text in real-time, displaying the translation on your screen. You can also take a photo of the text and highlight specific sections to translate.

Translating Websites

Step 1: Visit Google Translate. Go to translate.google.com in your web browser.

Step 2: Enter the website URL. Type or paste the URL of the website you want to translate into the left text box.

Step 3: Select languages. Choose the source language of the website and the target language for translation.

Step 4: Click on the translated link. Google Translate will generate a translated version of the website. Click on the link to view the translated website in a new tab.

Step 5: Browse the translated website. Navigate through the translated website as you would normally. Google Translate will continue to translate the content as you explore different pages.

Using Google Translate Offline

Step 1: Open the Google Translate app. Open the app on your mobile device.

Step 2: Download languages. Tap the menu icon (three horizontal lines) in the top left corner and select "Offline translation." Tap the download icon next to the languages you want to use offline.

Step 3: Use Google Translate offline. Once the languages are downloaded, you can use Google Translate without an internet connection. Enter text, use the camera, or speak into the app to get translations offline.

Additional Features

Step 1: Phrasebook. Save frequently used translations to your phrasebook for easy access later. Tap the star icon next to a translation to save it. Access your phrasebook by tapping the menu icon and selecting "Phrasebook."

Step 2: Handwriting. In the Google Translate app, you can draw characters or words that are not easily typed. Tap the pen icon to switch to handwriting mode and draw the characters on the screen.

Step 3: Conversation Mode. In the mobile app, you can use conversation mode for real-time, back-and-forth translations during a conversation. Tap the conversation icon and speak with the person. Google Translate will detect the languages being spoken and provide translations for both parties.

Step 4: Word Lens. Use the Word Lens feature in the mobile app to instantly translate printed text. Point your camera at signs, menus, or other printed materials, and see the translation overlaid on the original text.

Practical Examples

Example 1: Traveling Abroad. Suppose you are traveling in a foreign country and need to ask for directions. Open the Google Translate app, select your language and the local language, tap the microphone icon, and speak your question. Show the translated text to a local, or let them listen to the translation.

Example 2: Reading Foreign Documents. Suppose you have a document in a foreign language. Use the Google Translate app, tap the camera icon, and point your camera at the text. Google Translate will display the translation on your screen, making it easy to understand the document.

Example 3: Online Research. Suppose you come across a website in a foreign language while researching. Use Google Translate in your browser, enter the URL, and view the translated website to access the information you need.

Example 4: Learning a New Language. Suppose you are learning a new language and want to practice pronunciation. Use Google Translate to translate words and phrases, and tap the speaker icon to hear the correct pronunciation.

Google Calendar

Google Calendar is a powerful tool that helps you manage your schedule, set reminders, and coordinate with others. It is part of the Google Workspace suite and can be accessed from various devices, ensuring you stay organized and on top of your commitments.

Accessing Google Calendar on a Web Browser

Step 1: Open your web browser. Google Calendar is accessible from any web browser on your computer or mobile device.

Step 2: Visit the Google Calendar website. Type calendar.google.com into the address bar and press Enter. This will take you to the Google Calendar homepage.

Step 3: Sign in to your Google account. If you are not already signed in, you will be prompted to enter your Google account credentials. Enter your email address and password, then click "Next" to sign in. If you do not have a Google account, you can create one by clicking "Create account" and following the instructions.

Step 4: Explore the Google Calendar interface. Once signed in, you will see the main Google Calendar interface. The calendar view will display the current date and your scheduled events. The left sidebar allows you to navigate between different views (Day, Week, Month, Year, Schedule, 4 Days), create new events, and manage your calendars.

Accessing Google Calendar on a Mobile Device

Step 1: Download the Google Calendar app. If you do not already have the app, download it from the Google Play Store (for Android devices) or the Apple App Store (for iOS devices).

Step 2: Open the Google Calendar app. Tap the app icon on your home screen or app drawer to open Google Calendar.

Step 3: Sign in to your Google account. If you are not already signed in, you will be prompted to enter your Google account credentials. Enter your email address and password, then tap "Next" to sign in. If you do not have a Google account, you can create one by tapping "Create account" and following the instructions.

Step 4: Explore the Google Calendar interface. Once signed in, you will see the main Google Calendar interface. The calendar view will display the current date and your scheduled events. Use the bottom navigation bar to switch between different views (Day, 3 Day, Week, Month, Schedule), create new events, and access settings.

Step 1: Ensure synchronization is enabled. To keep your calendar up to date across all devices, ensure that synchronization is enabled. On your mobile device, go to your device's settings, select "Accounts," and ensure that Google Calendar synchronization is turned on.

Step 2: Access Google Calendar on other devices. Once synchronization is enabled, you can access Google Calendar from any device with an internet connection. Simply sign in to your Google account on the device, and your calendar events will automatically sync.

Adding Google Calendar to Your Desktop

Step 1: Create a desktop shortcut. To create a shortcut to Google Calendar on your desktop, open Google Calendar in your web browser.

Step 2: Use Chrome's shortcut feature. If you are using Google Chrome, click the three-dot menu icon in the top right corner, select "More tools," and then "Create shortcut." Check the "Open as window" box and click "Create." This will create a shortcut to Google Calendar on your desktop, allowing you to access it directly without opening your browser first.

Customize Your View

Google Calendar allows you to customize your view to better manage and organize your schedule. You can adjust the calendar display to suit your preferences and needs, making it easier to keep track of your events and tasks.

Changing the Calendar View

Step 1: Access Google Calendar. Open Google Calendar on your web browser by visiting calendar.google.com or open the Google Calendar app on your mobile device.

Step 2: Select the desired view. Google Calendar offers several view options: Day, Week, Month, Year, Schedule, and 4 Days. On the web, these options are located at the top right corner of the calendar. On mobile, you can access these views by tapping the menu icon (three horizontal lines) and selecting the desired view.

Step 3: Day View. The Day view displays your events for a single day, making it ideal for focusing on detailed daily planning. To switch to the Day view, click on "Day" at the top right corner of the calendar.

Step 4: Week View. The Week view shows your events for the entire week, providing a broader perspective of your schedule. To switch to the Week view, click on "Week."

Step 5: Month View. The Month view displays your events for the entire month, offering an overview of your long-term schedule. To switch to the Month view, click on "Month."

Step 6: Year View. The Year view allows you to see all your events for the entire year at a glance. This view is useful for long-term planning and identifying busy periods. To switch to the Year view, click on "Year."

Step 7: Schedule View. The Schedule view lists all your upcoming events in a linear format, making it easy to see what's coming up next. To switch to the Schedule view, click on "Schedule."

Step 8: 4 Days View. The 4 Days view shows your events over the next four days, providing a detailed yet short-term perspective of your schedule. To switch to the 4 Days view, click on "4 Days."

Adjusting Calendar Settings

Step 1: Open calendar settings. On the web, click on the gear icon in the top right corner and select "Settings." On mobile, tap the menu icon (three horizontal lines), scroll down, and tap "Settings."

Step 2: Customize your default view. In the settings menu, you can set your preferred default view by selecting "View options" on the web or "General" on mobile. Choose from Day, Week, Month, Year, Schedule, or 4 Days as your default view.

Step 3: Set custom work hours. If you have specific working hours, you can set them in the settings to prevent scheduling events outside your availability. In the settings menu, select "Working hours" and specify your workdays and hours.

Step 4: Enable or disable weekend display. You can choose whether to display weekends in your calendar view. In the settings menu, select "View options" and toggle the "Show weekends" option on or off.

Step 5: Customize event colors. Assign different colors to your events to differentiate between various types of activities. On the web, click on an event, then click the color palette icon to choose a color. On mobile, tap an event, then tap the color palette icon to select a color.

Step 6: Display additional calendars. You can display multiple calendars, such as your personal calendar, work calendar, and shared calendars, to see all your events in one place. In the left sidebar on the web or the menu on mobile, check the boxes next to the calendars you want to display.

Create an Event in Google Calendar

Creating events in Google Calendar is straightforward and allows you to schedule meetings, appointments, reminders, and other activities efficiently.

Creating an Event on a Web Browser

Step 1: Access Google Calendar. Open your web browser and go to calendar.google.com. Sign in to your Google account if you haven't already.

Step 2: Click on the desired date and time. In the calendar view, click on the date and time when you want to schedule the event. A pop-up window will appear where you can enter event details.

Step 3: Enter event details. In the pop-up window, you can:

- **Title:** Enter a title for your event to describe what it is.
- **Time:** Adjust the start and end times for your event. You can also set the event as an all-day event by checking the "All day" box.
- **Location:** Add a location for your event to provide attendees with the meeting place.
- **Description:** Add a description or notes about the event to provide additional details.

Step 4: Add guests. To invite others to your event, click on "Add guests" on the right side of the pop-up window and enter their email addresses. You can also set permissions for guests, such as allowing them to modify the event, invite others, or see the guest list.

Step 5: Set a notification. Set up a reminder for the event by clicking on the bell icon. You can choose when you want to be reminded (minutes, hours, days, or weeks before the event).

Step 6: Choose a calendar. If you have multiple calendars, select the one where you want to add the event by clicking on the calendar name next to the event title.

Step 7: Save the event. Click the "Save" button to add the event to your calendar. If you added guests, Google Calendar will prompt you to send invitations to them.

Creating an Event on a Mobile Device

Step 1: Open the Google Calendar app. Tap the Google Calendar app icon on your mobile device to open it.

Step 2: Tap the "Create" button. Tap the "+" button or the "Create" button (usually a colorful circle with a plus sign) at the bottom right corner of the screen.

Step 3: Enter event details. Fill in the necessary information for your event:

- **Title:** Enter the event title.
- **Date and Time:** Set the start and end times. You can also make it an all-day event by toggling the "All day" switch.
- **Location:** Add a location for the event.
- **Description:** Add any relevant details or notes about the event.

Step 4: Add guests. Tap the "Add people" field and enter the email addresses of the people you want to invite. Set their permissions as needed.

Step 5: Set a notification. Tap on "Add notification" to set a reminder for the event. Choose how far in advance you want to be notified.

Step 6: Choose a calendar. If you have multiple calendars, select the appropriate one by tapping the calendar name above the event title.

Step 7: Save the event. Tap the "Save" or "Done" button at the top right corner of the screen to add the event to your calendar. If you added guests, the app will prompt you to send invitations to them.

How to Create a Task in Google Calendar

Google Calendar is not only for scheduling events but also for managing tasks. Creating tasks in Google Calendar helps you keep track of your to-dos alongside your events, ensuring you stay organized and productive.

Creating a Task on a Web Browser

Step 1: Access Google Calendar. Open your web browser and go to calendar.google.com. Sign in to your Google account if you haven't already.

Step 2: Open the Tasks pane. On the right side of the Google Calendar interface, you will see a panel with icons for various Google apps. Click on the Tasks icon (a blue circle with a checkmark) to open the Tasks pane.

Step 3: Create a new task. Click on the "Add a task" button at the bottom of the Tasks pane. A text box will appear where you can enter the task details.

Step 4: Enter task details. In the text box, type the name of your task. Press Enter to save it. You can add more details by clicking on the task name, which opens a detailed view where you can add:

- **Description:** Additional information about the task.
- **Date and Time:** Set a due date and time for the task by clicking on "Add date/time."
- **Subtasks:** Break down the task into smaller steps by clicking on "Add subtasks" and entering the subtasks.

Step 5: Save the task. Once you have entered all the necessary details, click anywhere outside the task detail view to save your task. The task will now appear in your Tasks pane and, if you set a date, on your calendar.

Creating a Task on a Mobile Device

Step 1: Open the Google Calendar app. Tap the Google Calendar app icon on your mobile device to open it.

Step 2: Open the Create menu. Tap the "+" button or the "Create" button (usually a colorful circle with a plus sign) at the bottom right corner of the screen.

Step 3: Select "Task." In the Create menu, tap on "Task" to open the task creation screen.

Step 4: Enter task details. Fill in the necessary information for your task:

- **Title:** Enter the task name.
- **Date and Time:** Set the due date and time for the task by tapping on "Date" and "Time."
- **Description:** Add any additional details about the task in the description field.

Step 5: Save the task. Tap the "Save" button at the top right corner of the screen to add the task to your calendar. The task will now appear in your task list and on your calendar if you set a date.

Appointment Schedule

Creating an appointment schedule in Google Calendar allows you to set up blocks of time during which others can book appointments with you. This feature is particularly useful for managing office hours, consultations, meetings, or any other time-based services.

Creating an Appointment Schedule on a Web Browser

Step 1: Access Google Calendar. Open your web browser and go to calendar.google.com. Sign in to your Google account if you haven't already.

Step 2: Create a new event. Click on the date and time when you want to start your appointment schedule. A pop-up window will appear.

Step 3: Select "Appointment schedule." In the pop-up window, click on the "Appointment schedule" tab at the top. This will allow you to create a block of time that others can book appointments within.

Step 4: Set up your appointment schedule. Enter the necessary details for your appointment schedule:

- **Title:** Enter a title for your appointment schedule, such as "Office Hours" or "Consultations."
- **Date and Time:** Set the start and end times for your appointment schedule. You can also set it to repeat on specific days by clicking the "Does not repeat" dropdown and selecting your desired recurrence (e.g., weekly on Mondays and Wednesdays).

Step 5: Configure appointment slots. Set the duration of each appointment slot by entering the desired length of time (e.g., 30 minutes). You can also specify a buffer time between appointments if needed.

Step 6: Add location and details. Enter the location where the appointments will take place (e.g., office address or a video conferencing link). You can also add any additional details or instructions in the description field.

Step 7: Save the appointment schedule. Click "Save" to create the appointment schedule. Your appointment slots will now appear on your calendar.

Step 8: Share the booking link. After saving the appointment schedule, click on the appointment schedule event in your calendar. In the event details, you will find a link to the booking page. Copy this link and share it with those who need to book appointments with you.

Managing Your Appointment Schedule

Step 1: View booked appointments. Click on the appointment schedule event in your calendar to see which slots have been booked and by whom. You can also access this information from the appointment schedule's booking page.

Step 2: Modify or cancel appointments. If you need to modify or cancel any appointments, click on the booked slot in your calendar and make the necessary changes. You can reschedule or delete appointments as needed.

Step 3: Update your appointment schedule. If you need to change the availability of your appointment schedule, click on the appointment schedule event and edit the date, time, or duration of the appointment slots. Save the changes to update your schedule.

Managing Appointment Bookings

Managing appointment bookings in Google Calendar involves keeping track of who has booked appointments, modifying or canceling bookings, and ensuring your availability is accurately reflected.

Viewing and Tracking Booked Appointments

Step 1: Access Google Calendar. Open your web browser and go to calendar.google.com. Sign in to your Google account if you haven't already.

Step 2: Locate your appointment schedule. Find the appointment schedule on your calendar. It will be displayed as a block of time with the title you set (e.g., "Office Hours" or "Consultations").

Step 3: View booked slots. Click on the appointment schedule event to open the event details. Here, you can see which slots have been booked and the names or email addresses of the people who booked them.

Modifying Booked Appointments

Step 1: Select the booked slot. Click on the specific booked appointment slot within your appointment schedule. This will open the detailed view of that appointment.

Step 2: Edit appointment details. To change the date, time, or other details of the appointment, click on the "Edit" button (pencil icon). Make the necessary changes and click "Save." Google Calendar will notify the attendee of the changes.

Step 3: Reschedule an appointment. If you need to reschedule an appointment, edit the date and time fields in the appointment details. Click "Save" to update the booking. The attendee will be notified of the new appointment time.

Canceling Booked Appointments

Step 1: Select the booked slot. Click on the specific booked appointment slot within your appointment schedule.

Step 2: Open the appointment details. In the detailed view, click on the "More options" button (three vertical dots).

Step 3: Delete the appointment. Click on "Delete" to cancel the appointment. Google Calendar will ask if you want to notify the attendee. Choose to send a cancellation notification, so the attendee knows the appointment has been canceled.

Step 4: Confirm the deletion. Confirm that you want to delete the appointment. The slot will be removed from your calendar, and the attendee will be notified.

Managing Availability

Step 1: Update appointment schedule. To change your availability for future bookings, click on the appointment schedule event and select "Edit."

Step 2: Adjust dates and times. In the event details, update the dates, start and end times, or recurrence settings to reflect your new availability. Click "Save" to apply the changes.

Step 3: Notify existing bookings. If your changes affect existing bookings, consider notifying the attendees of the change or rescheduling their appointments manually.

Sharing your Google Calendar allows others to view or manage your schedule, facilitating better coordination and collaboration.

Sharing Your Calendar on a Web Browser

Step 1: Access Google Calendar. Open your web browser and go to calendar.google.com. Sign in to your Google account if you haven't already.

Step 2: Open calendar settings. In the left sidebar, find the calendar you want to share under the "My calendars" section. Hover over the calendar name, click the three vertical dots (More options) that appear, and select "Settings and sharing."

Step 3: Share with specific people. Scroll down to the "Share with specific people" section and click on "Add people."

Step 4: Enter email addresses. In the pop-up window, enter the email addresses of the people you want to share your calendar with. You can enter multiple email addresses separated by commas.

Step 5: Set permissions. Next to each email address, select the level of access you want to grant from the dropdown menu:

- **See only free/busy (hide details):** The person can see when your calendar is booked and when it's free, but not the details of your events.
- **See all event details:** The person can see all details of your events.
- **Make changes to events:** The person can see and modify your events.
- **Make changes and manage sharing:** The person has full access to your calendar, including the ability to share it with others.

Step 6: Send the invitation. Click "Send" to share your calendar. The recipients will receive an email notification with a link to add your calendar to their own Google Calendar.

Sharing Your Calendar on a Mobile Device

Step 1: Open the Google Calendar app. Tap the Google Calendar app icon on your mobile device to open it.

Step 2: Open calendar settings. Tap the menu icon (three horizontal lines) in the top left corner to open the sidebar menu. Scroll down and tap "Settings."

Step 3: Select the calendar to share. In the Settings menu, tap on the calendar you want to share.

Step 4: Add people. Tap "Share with specific people," then tap "Add people."

Step 5: Enter email addresses. Enter the email addresses of the people you want to share your calendar with, and set their permission levels.

Step 6: Send the invitation. Tap "Send" to share your calendar. The recipients will receive an email notification with a link to add your calendar to their own Google Calendar.

Setting up Alerts and Notifications

Setting up alerts and notifications in Google Calendar ensures you never miss an important event, meeting, or task. Google Calendar allows you to customize notifications to fit your preferences, including email alerts and pop-up notifications.

Step 1: Access Google Calendar. Open your web browser and go to calendar.google.com. Sign in to your Google account if you haven't already.

Step 2: Open calendar settings. In the left sidebar, find the calendar for which you want to set up notifications under the "My calendars" section. Hover over the calendar name, click the three vertical dots (More options) that appear, and select "Settings and sharing."

Step 3: Configure event notifications. Scroll down to the "Event notifications" section. Here, you can add, edit, or remove notifications:

- **Add a notification:** Click on "Add notification," choose whether you want a "Notification" or "Email," and set the time (e.g., 10 minutes, 1 hour, 1 day before the event). Click "Add" to save.
- **Edit a notification:** Click on the existing notification to change the type or timing.
- **Remove a notification:** Click the trash icon next to the notification you want to remove.

Step 4: Configure all-day event notifications. Scroll down to the "All-day event notifications" section. Similar to event notifications, you can add, edit, or remove notifications for all-day events.

Step 5: Save changes. Once you've configured your notifications, your settings will be saved automatically.

Setting Up Notifications for Individual Events

Step 1: Create or open an event. Click on the date and time of the event you want to set up notifications for, or click on an existing event to open it.

Step 2: Add notifications. In the event details, find the "Notification" section. Click on "Add notification" to add a new notification. Choose "Notification" or "Email" and set the desired time before the event.

Step 3: Customize notifications. You can add multiple notifications by clicking "Add notification" again and setting different times (e.g., one notification 30 minutes before and another 1 hour before).

Step 4: Save the event. After setting up the notifications, click "Save" to apply the changes to your event.

Setting Up Notifications on a Mobile Device

Step 1: Open the Google Calendar app. Tap the Google Calendar app icon on your mobile device to open it.

Step 2: Open calendar settings. Tap the menu icon (three horizontal lines) in the top left corner to open the sidebar menu. Scroll down and tap "Settings."

Step 3: Select the calendar to configure. Tap on the calendar for which you want to set up notifications.

Step 4: Configure event notifications. Tap "Event notifications" and then "Add notification." Choose the type of notification (Push Notification or Email) and set the time. Tap "Add" to save the notification.

Step 5: Configure all-day event notifications. Tap "All-day event notifications" and set the desired notification time (e.g., one day before, at 9 AM).

Color-Coding and Sub-Calendars

Google Calendar offers powerful features to help you organize and manage your schedule more effectively. Two key features are color-coding and sub-calendars, which allow you to visually differentiate between various types of events and manage different aspects of your life or work within the same calendar interface.

Using Color-Coding in Google Calendar

Color-coding helps you visually differentiate between different types of events, making it easier to see at a glance what your day or week looks like.

Step 1: Access Google Calendar. Open your web browser and go to calendar.google.com. Sign in to your Google account if you haven't already.

Step 2: Select an event. Click on an existing event or create a new event by clicking on the date and time in your calendar.

Step 3: Open event details. If you're creating a new event, fill in the necessary details. For an existing event, click on the event to open its details.

Step 4: Choose a color. Click on the color palette icon next to the event title. A selection of colors will appear. Choose a color that you want to assign to the event.

Step 5: Save the event. Click "Save" to apply the color to the event. The event will now be displayed in the chosen color in your calendar view.

Step 6: Color-coding multiple events. Repeat the process for other events. You can use different colors to categorize events, such as work, personal, meetings, deadlines, and more.

Creating and Managing Sub-Calendars

Sub-calendars allow you to manage different aspects of your schedule within separate calendars, all accessible from your main Google Calendar interface. This is useful for separating work from personal events, managing team schedules, or organizing specific projects.

Step 1: Access Google Calendar. Open your web browser and go to calendar.google.com. Sign in to your Google account if you haven't already.

Step 2: Create a new sub-calendar. In the left sidebar under the "My calendars" section, click the "+" (plus) icon next to "Add other calendars." Select "Create new calendar."

Step 3: Name your sub-calendar. Enter a name for your new sub-calendar, such as "Work," "Personal," "Team Projects," etc. Add a description and set the appropriate time zone.

Step 4: Create the sub-calendar. Click "Create calendar." Your new sub-calendar will now appear under the "My calendars" section in the left sidebar.

Step 5: Customize the sub-calendar. Click on the new sub-calendar's name in the left sidebar, then click the three vertical dots (More options) next to it. Choose a color for the sub-calendar to differentiate it from your other calendars.

Step 6: Add events to the sub-calendar. When creating a new event, choose the appropriate sub-calendar from the dropdown menu next to the event title. This will add the event to the selected sub-calendar, and it will be displayed in the color you chose.

Step 7: View and manage sub-calendars. You can toggle the visibility of each sub-calendar by checking or unchecking the box next to its name in the left sidebar. This allows you to focus on specific areas of your schedule without distraction.

Setting Goals and Managing Tasks

Setting goals and managing tasks in Google Calendar can help you stay organized and achieve your objectives efficiently.

Setting Goals in Google Calendar

Step 1: Access Google Calendar. Open your web browser and go to calendar.google.com. Sign in to your Google account if you haven't already.

Step 2: Open the Create menu. Click the "+ Create" button on the left side of the screen.

Step 3: Select "Goal." In the Create menu, click on "Goal." This will open the Goal setup menu.

Step 4: Choose a goal category. Select the category that best fits your goal, such as Exercise, Build a Skill, Family & Friends, Me Time, or Organize My Life.

Step 5: Select a specific goal. Choose a specific goal within the selected category. For example, under Exercise, you might choose "Work out."

Step 6: Set the frequency. Specify how often you want to work on this goal. Options include daily, weekly, or custom frequencies.

Step 7: Set the duration. Choose how long you want to spend on this goal each time. Options include 15 minutes, 30 minutes, 1 hour, etc.

Step 8: Choose the best time. Select the best time for Google Calendar to schedule your goal. Options include morning, afternoon, evening, or "Any time."

Step 9: Create the goal. Click "Done" to create the goal. Google Calendar will automatically find the best time to schedule your goal based on your availability.

Managing Tasks in Google Calendar

Step 1: Access Google Calendar. Open your web browser and go to calendar.google.com. Sign in to your Google account if you haven't already.

Step 2: Open the Tasks pane. In the right-hand side panel, click on the Tasks icon (a blue circle with a checkmark) to open the Tasks pane.

Step 3: Create a new task. Click on the "Add a task" button at the bottom of the Tasks pane. A text box will appear for you to enter the task details.

Step 4: Enter task details. Type the name of your task in the text box and press Enter to save it. To add more details, click on the task name to open the detailed view.

Step 5: Add a description. In the task detail view, add a description or notes about the task if needed.

Step 6: Set a due date and time. Click on "Add date/time" to set a due date and time for the task. This will make the task appear on your calendar.

Step 7: Create subtasks. If the task can be broken down into smaller steps, click on "Add subtasks" and enter the subtasks.

Step 8: Save the task. Click anywhere outside the task detail view to save the task. The task will now appear in your Tasks pane and on your calendar if a date is set.

Managing Tasks on a Mobile Device

Step 1: Open the Google Calendar app. Tap the Google Calendar app icon on your mobile device to open it.

Step 2: Open the Create menu. Tap the "+" button or the "Create" button (usually a colorful circle with a plus sign) at the bottom right corner of the screen.

Step 3: Select "Task." In the Create menu, tap on "Task" to open the task creation screen.

Step 4: Enter task details. Fill in the necessary information for your task, such as the title and description.

Step 5: Set a due date and time. Tap on "Date" and "Time" to set the due date and time for the task.

Step 6: Save the task. Tap the "Save" button at the top right corner of the screen to add the task to your calendar. The task will now appear in your task list and on your calendar if a date is set.

Managing Recurring Events

Google Calendar allows you to set up recurring events for activities that happen regularly, such as weekly meetings, monthly reviews, or annual events. This feature helps you stay organized by automatically scheduling these events.

Creating Recurring Events on a Web Browser

Step 1: Access Google Calendar. Open your web browser and go to calendar.google.com. Sign in to your Google account if you haven't already.

Step 2: Create a new event. Click on the date and time when you want to start the recurring event. A pop-up window will appear.

Step 3: Enter event details. In the pop-up window, enter the event title, location, and any other details.

Step 4: Set the event as recurring. Click on the "Does not repeat" dropdown menu to open the recurrence options.

Step 5: Choose a recurrence pattern. Select the appropriate recurrence pattern for your event:

- **Daily:** The event will occur every day.
- **Weekly:** The event will occur on the same day every week.
- **Monthly:** The event will occur on the same date every month.
- **Yearly:** The event will occur on the same date every year.
- **Custom:** Allows you to set a custom recurrence pattern (e.g., every 2 weeks, every 3 months).

Step 6: Set the end date. If applicable, set an end date for the recurrence by choosing "Ends on" and selecting a date, or set it to "Ends after" a certain number of occurrences.

Step 7: Save the event. Click "Save" to create the recurring event. The event will now appear on your calendar according to the chosen recurrence pattern.

Editing Recurring Events

Step 1: Select the recurring event. Click on any instance of the recurring event in your calendar to open the event details.

Step 2: Click "Edit event." Click the pencil icon to open the event editing window.

Step 3: Make changes. Update the event details as needed (e.g., changing the time, location, or description).

Step 4: Save changes. Click "Save." A prompt will ask if you want to apply the changes to just this event, all events, or all following events in the series. Choose the appropriate option.

Deleting Recurring Events

Step 1: Select the recurring event. Click on any instance of the recurring event in your calendar to open the event details.

Step 2: Click "Delete." Click the trash icon to delete the event.

Step 3: Confirm deletion. A prompt will ask if you want to delete just this event, all events, or all following events in the series. Choose the appropriate option to confirm deletion.

Managing Recurring Events on a Mobile Device

Step 1: Open the Google Calendar app. Tap the Google Calendar app icon on your mobile device to open it.

Step 2: Create a new event. Tap the "+" button or the "Create" button (usually a colorful circle with a plus sign) at the bottom right corner of the screen.

Step 3: Enter event details. Fill in the necessary information for your event, such as the title, location, and description.

Step 4: Set the event as recurring. Tap "Does not repeat" to open the recurrence options.

Step 5: Choose a recurrence pattern. Select the appropriate recurrence pattern for your event:

- **Daily:** The event will occur every day.
- **Weekly:** The event will occur on the same day every week.
- **Monthly:** The event will occur on the same date every month.
- **Yearly:** The event will occur on the same date every year.
- **Custom:** Allows you to set a custom recurrence pattern (e.g., every 2 weeks, every 3 months).

Step 6: Set the end date. If applicable, set an end date for the recurrence by choosing "Ends on" and selecting a date, or set it to "Ends after" a certain number of occurrences.

Step 7: Save the event. Tap the "Save" button at the top right corner of the screen to create the recurring event. The event will now appear on your calendar according to the chosen recurrence pattern.

Editing and Deleting Recurring Events on a Mobile Device

Step 1: Select the recurring event. Tap on any instance of the recurring event in your calendar to open the event details.

Step 2: Edit the event. Tap the pencil icon to open the event editing screen. Make the necessary changes and tap "Save." Choose to apply the changes to just this event, all events, or all following events in the series.

Step 3: Delete the event. Tap the trash icon to delete the event. Choose to delete just this event, all events, or all following events in the series.

Google Tasks

Google Tasks is a simple yet powerful tool integrated within Google Workspace that helps you manage your to-do lists and keep track of tasks across your devices.

Step 1: Open Google Tasks. To access Google Tasks, open your web browser and go to mail.google.com or calendar.google.com. Google Tasks is integrated within Gmail and Google Calendar.

Step 2: Sign in to your Google account. If you haven't already, sign in to your Google account using your email and password.

Step 3: Open the Tasks pane. In Gmail, click on the "Tasks" icon (a blue circle with a checkmark) in the right-hand sidebar. In Google Calendar, the Tasks pane is also accessible from the right-hand sidebar.

Step 4: View and manage tasks. The Tasks pane will display your task lists and tasks. You can view, add, edit, and complete tasks directly from this pane.

Accessing Google Tasks on a Mobile Device

Step 1: Download the Google Tasks app. If you do not have the Google Tasks app, download it from the Google Play Store (for Android devices) or the Apple App Store (for iOS devices).

Step 2: Open the Google Tasks app. Tap the Google Tasks app icon on your mobile device to open it.

Step 3: Sign in to your Google account. If prompted, sign in to your Google account using your email and password.

Step 4: View and manage tasks. The Google Tasks app will display your task lists and tasks. You can view, add, edit, and complete tasks from the app.

Creating and Managing Tasks

Step 1: Create a new task. In the Tasks pane (on the web) or in the Google Tasks app (on mobile), click or tap on "Add a task." A text box will appear for you to enter the task details.

Step 2: Enter task details. Type the name of your task in the text box and press Enter to save it. To add more details, click on the task name to open the detailed view.

Step 3: Add a description. In the task detail view, add a description or notes about the task if needed.

Step 4: Set a due date and time. Click on "Add date/time" to set a due date and time for the task. This will make the task appear on your calendar.

Step 5: Create subtasks. If the task can be broken down into smaller steps, click on "Add subtasks" and enter the subtasks.

Step 6: Save the task. Click anywhere outside the task detail view to save the task. The task will now appear in your Tasks pane and on your calendar if a date is set.

Organizing Tasks

Step 1: Create task lists. To create a new task list, click or tap on "Create new list" in the Tasks pane or app. Enter a name for the list and press Enter to save it.

Step 2: Move tasks between lists. To move a task to a different list, open the task detail view and select the desired list from the dropdown menu.

Step 3: Sort and filter tasks. You can sort tasks by date or reorder them manually. In the Tasks pane or app, use the sort options to organize your tasks as needed.

Completing and Deleting Tasks

Step 1: Mark tasks as complete. To mark a task as complete, click or tap the checkbox next to the task name. Completed tasks will be moved to the "Completed" section of your task list.

Step 2: Delete tasks. To delete a task, open the task detail view and click or tap on the trash icon. Confirm the deletion to remove the task from your list.

Synchronizing Tasks Across Devices

Step 1: Ensure synchronization is enabled. Google Tasks automatically syncs across all devices connected to your Google account. Make sure you are signed in to the same account on all devices.

Step 2: Access tasks from different devices. You can access and manage your tasks from any device with Google Tasks, Gmail, or Google Calendar.

Google Tasks is seamlessly integrated into both Gmail and Google Calendar, allowing you to manage your tasks alongside your emails and calendar events. This integration helps streamline your workflow and ensures that your tasks are always accessible.

Using Google Tasks in Gmail

Step 1: Open Gmail. Go to mail.google.com in your web browser and sign in to your Google account if you haven't already.

Step 2: Access the Tasks pane. In the right-hand sidebar of the Gmail interface, click on the "Tasks" icon (a blue circle with a checkmark). This will open the Google Tasks pane.

Step 3: View your tasks. The Tasks pane will display your task lists and individual tasks. You can scroll through your tasks, view details, and see which tasks are due soon.

Step 4: Create a new task. To create a new task, click on the "Add a task" button at the bottom of the Tasks pane. A text box will appear for you to enter the task details. Press Enter to save the task.

Step 5: Add task details. Click on a task to open its detail view. Here, you can add a description, set a due date and time, and create subtasks if necessary.

Step 6: Manage your tasks. You can mark tasks as complete by clicking the checkbox next to the task name. To delete a task, open the task detail view and click the trash icon.

Step 7: Convert emails into tasks. You can convert an email into a task by opening the email, clicking the three-dot menu icon at the top of the email, and selecting "Add to Tasks." The email will be added to your task list, and you can set additional details as needed.

Using Google Tasks in Google Calendar

Step 1: Open Google Calendar. Go to calendar.google.com in your web browser and sign in to your Google account if you haven't already.

Step 2: Access the Tasks pane. In the right-hand sidebar of the Google Calendar interface, click on the "Tasks" icon (a blue circle with a checkmark). This will open the Google Tasks pane.

Step 3: View your tasks. The Tasks pane will display your task lists and individual tasks. You can scroll through your tasks, view details, and see which tasks are due soon.

Step 4: Create a new task. To create a new task, click on the "Add a task" button at the bottom of the Tasks pane. A text box will appear for you to enter the task details. Press Enter to save the task.

Step 5: Add task details. Click on a task to open its detail view. Here, you can add a description, set a due date and time, and create subtasks if necessary.

Step 6: Manage your tasks. You can mark tasks as complete by clicking the checkbox next to the task name. To delete a task, open the task detail view and click the trash icon.

Step 7: View tasks on your calendar. Tasks with due dates will appear on your Google Calendar. You can see your tasks alongside your events and appointments, making it easier to manage your schedule.

Synchronizing Tasks Between Gmail and Google Calendar

Step 1: Ensure synchronization is enabled. Google Tasks automatically syncs between Gmail and Google Calendar as long as you are signed in to the same Google account on both services.

Step 2: Access tasks from either service. You can create, view, and manage tasks from either Gmail or Google Calendar. Changes made in one service will be reflected in the other.

Step 3: Use the mobile apps. Download the Google Tasks app on your mobile device to access and manage your tasks on the go. The app syncs with both Gmail and Google Calendar, ensuring that your tasks are always up to date.

Organizing Tasks

Step 1: Create task lists. You can create multiple task lists to organize your tasks by project, priority, or category. In the Tasks pane, click on "Create new list," enter a name for the list, and press Enter to save it.

Step 2: Move tasks between lists. To move a task to a different list, open the task detail view and select the desired list from the dropdown menu.

Step 3: Sort and filter tasks. Use the sort options in the Tasks pane to organize your tasks by date, name, or custom order.

Google Meet

Google Meet is a video conferencing tool that allows you to connect with others through video calls and meetings. It is part of the Google Workspace suite and offers a range of features to facilitate virtual meetings, webinars, and remote collaboration.

Step 1: Access Google Meet. You can access Google Meet in several ways:

- **Web Browser:** Go to meet.google.com in your web browser.
- **Gmail:** Open Gmail and click on the "Meet" section in the sidebar.
- **Google Calendar:** Open Google Calendar and create or join a meeting.
- **Mobile App:** Download the Google Meet app from the Google Play Store (Android) or Apple App Store (iOS).

Step 2: Sign in to your Google account. If you haven't already, sign in to your Google account using your email and password.

Starting a New Meeting

Step 1: Open Google Meet. Go to meet.google.com or open the Google Meet app on your mobile device.

Step 2: Click on "New meeting." On the homepage, click on the "New meeting" button. You'll have three options:

- **Create a meeting for later:** This generates a meeting link that you can share and use later.
- **Start an instant meeting:** This starts a meeting immediately.
- **Schedule in Google Calendar:** This opens Google Calendar to schedule a meeting for a future date and time.

Step 3: Join the meeting. If you chose to start an instant meeting, you will be taken directly to the meeting. If you created a meeting for later, share the meeting link with participants. If you scheduled a meeting in Google Calendar, the meeting link will be included in the calendar event.

Joining a Meeting

Step 1: Receive an invitation. You can join a Google Meet meeting through a link shared with you via email, calendar invite, or messaging app.

Step 2: Click the meeting link. Click on the meeting link to open Google Meet in your web browser or app.

Step 3: Join the meeting. Enter your name if prompted, and click "Join now" or "Ask to join." If the meeting organizer needs to admit you, wait for them to do so.

Managing Meeting Participants

Step 1: Open the participants pane. In the meeting window, click on the "People" icon to see the list of participants.

Step 2: Invite others. Click on "Add people" and enter the email addresses of the people you want to invite. Click "Send invite."

Step 3: Manage participants. You can mute, remove, or pin participants by clicking on their name in the participants pane and selecting the appropriate action.

Using Meeting Controls

Step 1: Mute/unmute microphone. Click on the microphone icon at the bottom of the meeting window to mute or unmute your microphone.

Step 2: Turn on/off camera. Click on the camera icon at the bottom of the meeting window to turn your camera on or off.

Step 3: Share your screen. Click on the "Present now" button at the bottom of the meeting window. Choose whether to share your entire screen, a window, or a specific tab.

Step 4: Use chat. Click on the chat icon to open the chat pane. Here, you can send messages to all participants.

Step 5: Record the meeting. If you have the necessary permissions, click on the three-dot menu (More options) and select "Record meeting." To stop recording, click on the three-dot menu again and select "Stop recording." The recording will be saved to your Google Drive.

Step 6: End the meeting. To leave the meeting, click on the red phone icon at the bottom of the meeting window. If you are the host and want to end the meeting for everyone, ensure all participants have left before you do.

Using Google Meet in Google Calendar

Step 1: Schedule a meeting. Open Google Calendar and click on the "Create" button to schedule a new event.

Step 2: Add Google Meet video conferencing. In the event details, click on "Add video conferencing" and select "Google Meet." A meeting link will be generated and included in the calendar event.

Step 3: Invite participants. Add the email addresses of the people you want to invite in the "Guests" section. They will receive an email with the event details and the Google Meet link.

Step 4: Join the meeting. At the scheduled time, click on the Google Meet link in the calendar event to join the meeting.

Using Google Meet on Mobile Devices

Step 1: Open the Google Meet app. Tap the Google Meet app icon on your mobile device to open it.

Step 2: Sign in to your Google account. If prompted, sign in using your email and password.

Step 3: Start or join a meeting. Tap on "New meeting" to start a meeting or "Meeting code" to join an existing meeting by entering the code provided.

Step 4: Use meeting controls. The meeting controls on mobile are similar to those on the web. You can mute/unmute your microphone, turn your camera on/off, share your screen, and use chat.

Features of Google Meet

Google Meet is a robust video conferencing platform that offers a wide range of features designed to facilitate remote meetings, webinars, and virtual collaborations.

High-Quality Video and Audio

HD Video: Google Meet supports high-definition video calls, ensuring clear and crisp video quality for a better meeting experience.

Noise Cancellation: Advanced noise cancellation technology filters out background noise, allowing participants to hear each other clearly, even in noisy environments.

Adaptive Layouts: Google Meet offers multiple layout options, including Auto, Tiled, Spotlight, and Sidebar, that automatically adjust to highlight the active speaker or show multiple participants at once.

Easy Accessibility

Web-Based Access: Google Meet can be accessed directly from a web browser without the need to download any additional software, making it convenient for users on different devices.

Mobile App: The Google Meet app, available for Android and iOS devices, allows users to join meetings on the go.

Integration with Google Workspace: Google Meet integrates seamlessly with other Google Workspace apps like Gmail and Google Calendar, enabling users to schedule, join, and manage meetings directly from these platforms.

Security and Privacy

Encrypted Meetings: All video meetings on Google Meet are encrypted in transit, ensuring that your conversations remain private and secure.

Two-Step Verification: Users can enable two-step verification for their Google accounts to add an extra layer of security.

Access Controls: Meeting hosts have control over who can join the meeting and can mute or remove participants if necessary.

Collaboration Tools

Screen Sharing: Participants can share their entire screen, a specific window, or a tab, making it easy to present documents, slides, and other content during meetings.

Real-Time Captions: Google Meet offers real-time captions powered by Google's speech recognition technology, making meetings more accessible for participants with hearing impairments.

Chat: An integrated chat feature allows participants to send messages during the meeting, facilitating communication without interrupting the speaker.

File Sharing: Participants can share files directly within the meeting by attaching them in the chat, making it easy to distribute important documents.

Meeting Management

Schedule and Join Meetings: Users can schedule meetings in advance using Google Calendar and join meetings directly from the calendar event or via a meeting link.

Recording: Meeting hosts can record meetings, including the audio, video, and screen sharing, and save them to Google Drive for later viewing.

Breakout Rooms: Hosts can create breakout rooms to divide participants into smaller groups for discussions or activities and then bring everyone back to the main meeting.

Polling and Q&A: Hosts can create polls and enable Q&A sessions during meetings to engage participants and gather feedback.

Customization and Flexibility

Virtual Backgrounds: Users can choose from a selection of virtual backgrounds or upload their own to customize their video feed.

Live Streaming: Google Meet supports live streaming of meetings to up to 100,000 viewers within a domain, making it ideal for large events and webinars.

Attendance Tracking: Hosts can track attendance during meetings, which is useful for educational and corporate environments to monitor participation.

Companion Mode: Companion mode allows users to join meetings from a second device for a richer experience, such as using one device for video and another for screen sharing or note-taking.

Performance and Reliability

Adaptive Bandwidth: Google Meet adjusts video and audio quality based on the participant's internet connection to provide the best possible experience even on low bandwidth.

Low Latency: The platform is optimized for low latency, ensuring minimal delays during conversations and screen sharing.

Scalability: Google Meet can accommodate up to 250 participants in a single meeting for Google Workspace Essentials, Business, and Enterprise customers.

By leveraging these key features, Google Meet provides a comprehensive and user-friendly solution for virtual meetings and collaboration. Whether you are conducting business meetings, teaching classes, or hosting webinars, Google Meet's robust feature set ensures that you can connect and communicate effectively with your audience.

Tips for Using Google Meet

Google Meet is a powerful tool for virtual meetings and collaboration, but to get the most out of it, there are several best practices and tips you can follow.

Preparing for a Meeting

Check Your Equipment: Ensure your camera, microphone, and speakers are working correctly before the meeting starts. Perform a quick test call to check audio and video quality.

Stable Internet Connection: Use a reliable internet connection to avoid disruptions. If possible, connect to a wired network for a more stable connection.

Quiet Environment: Choose a quiet location for your meeting to minimize background noise. Inform others around you to reduce interruptions.

Good Lighting: Ensure you are well-lit by positioning a light source in front of you. Avoid having bright lights or windows directly behind you, as they can cause shadows and make it difficult for others to see you.

During the Meeting

Mute When Not Speaking: To reduce background noise and avoid interruptions, keep your microphone muted when you are not speaking. Unmute only when you need to contribute.

Use Headphones: Using headphones can help improve audio quality and reduce echo or feedback during the call.

Engage with the Camera: Look into the camera when speaking to create a more personal connection with participants.

Utilize Chat and Reactions: Use the chat feature to share links, files, or comments without interrupting the speaker. Use reactions (like raising your hand) to signal that you want to speak or to show agreement.

Share Screen Effectively: When sharing your screen, close unnecessary tabs and applications to avoid distractions. Clearly narrate what you are presenting to keep participants engaged.

Use Virtual Backgrounds: If your background is distracting or you want more privacy, use virtual backgrounds. Choose a simple, professional image to maintain a clean appearance.

Record Important Meetings: If you need to review the meeting later or share it with those who couldn't attend, use the recording feature. Remember to inform participants that the meeting is being recorded.

Managing Participants

Admit Participants: As the host, you will need to admit participants from the waiting room. Be prompt to ensure the meeting starts on time.

Control Participation: Use the mute and remove options to manage disruptive participants. You can also lock the meeting to prevent new participants from joining after it starts.

Breakout Rooms: Use breakout rooms for group discussions or activities. Plan the breakout sessions in advance and provide clear instructions to participants.

Polling and Q&A: Use polls to gather quick feedback or opinions from participants. Enable Q&A to allow participants to ask questions without interrupting the flow of the meeting.

Post-Meeting

Share Meeting Notes: After the meeting, share notes or a summary with participants to ensure everyone is aligned on key points and action items.

Follow Up: Send follow-up emails or messages to address any unanswered questions or to provide additional information discussed during the meeting.

Review Recordings: If the meeting was recorded, review the recording to capture any missed details and to provide feedback for improvement in future meetings.

Advanced Tips

Companion Mode: Use companion mode to join meetings from a second device. This allows you to use one device for video and another for screen sharing or note-taking.

Live Streaming: For large events, use the live streaming feature to broadcast the meeting to a wider audience. This is useful for webinars and public announcements.

Customize Layouts: Adjust the layout settings to focus on the active speaker or to see all participants. Choose the layout that best suits your meeting type.

Explore Integrations: Google Meet integrates with other Google Workspace apps. Use these integrations to streamline your workflow. For example, schedule meetings directly from Google Calendar or start a Meet call from a Gmail thread.

Accessibility Features: Utilize accessibility features like live captions to make your meetings more inclusive for participants with hearing impairments.

Google Jamboard

Google Jamboard is an interactive, cloud-based whiteboard tool that enhances collaboration and creativity. It is part of the Google Workspace suite and offers a range of features designed to facilitate brainstorming, planning, teaching, and remote teamwork. Here are various uses of Google Jamboard and how it can be integrated into different scenarios.

1. Brainstorming Sessions

Interactive Brainstorming: Google Jamboard allows teams to brainstorm ideas in real-time. Participants can add sticky notes, draw, and write on the board simultaneously, making it easy to capture everyone's input.

Visual Collaboration: Use the drawing tools, shapes, and images to create mind maps, flowcharts, and diagrams. This visual approach helps in organizing thoughts and fostering creativity.

Remote Participation: Team members can join a Jamboard session from different locations, making it ideal for remote teams. The cloud-based nature of Jamboard ensures that everyone sees updates in real-time.

2. Project Planning

Task Management: Break down projects into tasks and assign them using sticky notes. Use different colors to categorize tasks and track progress visually.

Timelines and Roadmaps: Create timelines and roadmaps to plan project milestones and deadlines. Use shapes and arrows to indicate dependencies and flow.

Collaboration on Documentation: Team members can collaboratively edit and annotate documents, spreadsheets, and presentations linked to the Jamboard, ensuring everyone is aligned on project deliverables.

3. Teaching and Learning

Interactive Lessons: Teachers can use Jamboard to create interactive lessons. They can write notes, draw diagrams, and insert images or videos to make the lessons more engaging.

Student Collaboration: Students can work together on projects and assignments. They can brainstorm ideas, create mind maps, and share their work with classmates and teachers.

Real-Time Feedback: Teachers can provide real-time feedback by annotating students' work directly on the Jamboard. This immediate feedback helps students understand and correct mistakes.

4. Meetings and Workshops

Facilitating Discussions: Use Jamboard to facilitate discussions during meetings and workshops. Participants can add their thoughts and ideas in real-time, making the sessions more interactive.

Problem-Solving: Collaboratively solve problems by sketching out solutions on the board. Use different tools to highlight key points and visualize complex concepts.

Decision-Making: Use Jamboard to list options, weigh pros and cons, and make decisions collectively. The visual representation of information helps in better decision-making.

5. Creative Design and Prototyping

Design Sketches: Designers can use Jamboard to sketch out design ideas and concepts. The intuitive drawing tools allow for quick and easy creation of visual elements.

Collaborative Prototyping: Team members can work together on prototypes, providing input and making changes in real-time. This collaborative approach speeds up the design process.

Feedback and Iteration: Share design drafts on Jamboard and collect feedback from stakeholders. Iterate on designs based on the feedback, ensuring the final product meets everyone's expectations.

6. Strategic Planning

SWOT Analysis: Conduct SWOT (Strengths, Weaknesses, Opportunities, Threats) analysis on Jamboard. Use different sections of the board to categorize and visualize each element.

Business Model Canvas: Create a business model canvas to plan and develop business strategies. Fill in the different sections with ideas and collaborate with team members to refine the model.

Goal Setting and Tracking: Set organizational goals and track progress using Jamboard. Use sticky notes to outline goals and update the board regularly to reflect progress.

7. Training and Onboarding

Training Sessions: Use Jamboard to deliver training sessions. Trainers can illustrate concepts, write notes, and interact with trainees in real-time.

Interactive Onboarding: Onboard new employees by walking them through processes and workflows on Jamboard. Use visual aids to make the information more digestible.

Knowledge Sharing: Create a collaborative space for knowledge sharing. Team members can contribute resources, best practices, and tips, making it a valuable reference tool.

8. Personal Productivity

To-Do Lists: Create to-do lists and prioritize tasks on Jamboard. Use sticky notes to list tasks and organize them by priority or deadline.

Mind Mapping: Use Jamboard for personal brainstorming and mind mapping. Visualize your thoughts and ideas to help with planning and decision-making.

Goal Tracking: Set personal goals and track progress visually. Use different colors and shapes to represent various goals and milestones.

Integration with Google Workspace

Seamless Integration: Google Jamboard integrates seamlessly with other Google Workspace apps like Google Drive, Google Docs, and Google Calendar. This integration enhances productivity by allowing easy access to documents, scheduling, and collaboration.

Real-Time Collaboration: Team members can collaborate in real-time, no matter where they are. Changes are instantly visible to everyone, making remote work more efficient.

Cloud Storage: All Jamboard sessions are saved in Google Drive, ensuring they are accessible from anywhere and can be easily shared with others.

Basics of Google Jamboard

Google Jamboard is an interactive, cloud-based whiteboard tool designed to enhance collaboration and creativity among teams. It allows users to create and share visual content in real-time, making it a valuable asset for brainstorming sessions, project planning, teaching, and remote teamwork.

Getting Started with Google Jamboard

Step 1: Access Google Jamboard. You can access Jamboard in several ways:

- **Web Browser:** Go to jamboard.google.com.
- **Mobile App:** Download the Google Jamboard app from the Google Play Store (for Android) or the Apple App Store (for iOS).
- **Physical Jamboard Device:** If your organization has a physical Jamboard device, you can use it directly.

Step 2: Sign in to your Google account. If you haven't already, sign in to your Google account using your email and password.

Step 3: Create a new Jam. Click on the "+" (plus) button or "New Jam" to create a new Jamboard file. This will open a blank canvas where you can start your work.

Understanding the Jamboard Interface

Toolbar: The toolbar on the left side of the screen provides various tools for creating and editing content:

- **Pen Tool:** Allows you to draw and write on the canvas. You can choose different pen types (pen, marker, highlighter, brush) and colors.
- **Eraser Tool:** Use this to erase any mistakes or unwanted marks on the canvas.
- **Select Tool:** Allows you to select and move objects around the canvas.
- **Sticky Notes:** Add sticky notes to the canvas for quick notes or comments. You can choose different colors for the notes.
- **Images:** Insert images from your computer, Google Drive, or by searching the web.
- **Shapes:** Add various shapes (circles, squares, triangles, etc.) to the canvas.
- **Text Boxes:** Add text boxes to type and format text on the canvas.
- **Laser Pointer:** Use the laser pointer to highlight or draw attention to specific areas during a presentation.

Pages: At the top of the screen, you can add, delete, and navigate between multiple pages in a single Jamboard file. This allows you to organize your content across different pages.

Collaborators: Click on the "Share" button to invite others to collaborate on your Jam. You can add their email addresses and set permissions (view or edit).

Basic Functions of Google Jamboard

Drawing and Writing: Use the pen tool to draw or write on the canvas. Select different pen types and colors to differentiate your content.

Adding Sticky Notes: Click on the sticky note icon, type your note, choose a color, and click "Save." You can move and resize sticky notes as needed.

Inserting Images: Click on the image icon and choose an image source. You can upload images from your computer, select from Google Drive, or search the web. Insert the image and adjust its size and position on the canvas.

Adding Shapes and Text: Use the shapes tool to add geometric shapes. Click on the text box icon to add and format text. You can change the font size, style, and color.

Navigating Pages: Use the page navigation controls at the top to switch between different pages in your Jam. You can add new pages by clicking the "+" button or delete pages as needed.

Collaborating in Real-Time: Invite collaborators by clicking the "Share" button. Enter their email addresses and set their permissions. All changes made by collaborators are visible in real-time.

Using Google Jamboard for Different Purposes

Brainstorming: Use sticky notes, drawings, and text to brainstorm ideas. Collaborators can add their input simultaneously, making it a dynamic and interactive session.

Project Planning: Organize tasks, timelines, and resources visually. Use different pages for different aspects of the project and invite team members to collaborate.

Teaching: Create interactive lessons with drawings, images, and text. Students can join the Jamboard session and participate actively by adding their notes and ideas.

Remote Meetings: Use Jamboard to facilitate discussions and visualize concepts during remote meetings. Share the Jamboard with all participants and collaborate in real-time.

Tips for Effective Use of Google Jamboard

Organize Your Content: Use multiple pages to keep your content organized. Label each page clearly so you can navigate easily.

Color Code: Use different colors for sticky notes, text, and drawings to categorize information and make the content visually appealing.

Practice with Tools: Spend time familiarizing yourself with the different tools available in Jamboard. This will help you use the tool more efficiently during actual sessions.

Save and Share: Always save your Jams and share them with collaborators. Use the sharing settings to control who can view and edit your content.

Google Keep

Google Keep is a versatile and easy-to-use note-taking application that helps you capture and organize your thoughts, tasks, and reminders. Integrated seamlessly with Google Workspace, Google Keep allows you to create, edit, and collaborate on notes from any device.

Getting Started

Step 1: Access Google Keep. You can access Google Keep in several ways:

- **Web Browser:** Go to keep.google.com.
- **Mobile App:** Download the Google Keep app from the Google Play Store (for Android) or the Apple App Store (for iOS).
- **Google Workspace:** Access Google Keep from the sidebar in Google Workspace apps like Gmail, Google Docs, and Google Calendar.

Step 2: Sign in to your Google account. If you haven't already, sign in to your Google account using your email and password.

Step 3: Create a new note. Click on the "Take a note" field at the top of the page or tap the "+" button on the mobile app to create a new note. Enter your note's title and content.

Key Features of Google Keep

Text Notes: Create text notes to capture your thoughts, ideas, and reminders. Simply type your content into the note field and save it.

Checklists: Create checklists for tasks, grocery lists, or any other items you need to keep track of. Use the checkbox icon to add checkboxes to your note.

Voice Notes: Record voice notes by clicking the microphone icon (mobile app) and speaking into your device. Google Keep will transcribe the audio into text and attach the recording to your note.

Image Notes: Add images to your notes by clicking the image icon and uploading a photo from your device or taking a new one with your camera (mobile app).

Drawing Notes: Use the drawing tool to create sketches or handwritten notes. Click on the brush icon to open the drawing canvas.

Reminders: Set reminders for your notes by clicking the reminder icon. You can choose a specific date and time or set location-based reminders that notify you when you arrive at a particular place.

Labels: Organize your notes with labels. Click on the label icon and create or select labels to categorize your notes. This helps you quickly find related notes.

Color Coding: Assign different colors to your notes to differentiate them visually. Click on the color palette icon and choose a color for your note.

Pinning Notes: Pin important notes to the top of your list by clicking the pin icon. Pinned notes remain at the top for easy access.

Archiving Notes: Archive notes you don't need immediately but want to keep for future reference. Click the archive icon to move a note to the archive section.

Collaborating on Notes: Share notes with others to collaborate in real-time. Click the collaborator icon, enter the email addresses of the people you want to share with, and set their permissions.

Using Google Keep for Different Purposes

Task Management: Use checklists and reminders to manage your tasks. Create separate notes for different projects or categories and use labels to organize them.

Brainstorming: Capture ideas and inspiration as they come to you. Use text, images, and drawings to create comprehensive brainstorming notes.

Project Planning: Plan projects by creating notes for each phase or task. Use checklists to track progress and set reminders for deadlines.

Meeting Notes: Take notes during meetings and share them with attendees. Use labels to categorize notes by meeting topics or projects.

Personal Organization: Use Google Keep for personal organization, such as keeping track of recipes, shopping lists, or fitness goals.

Creative Writing: Jot down story ideas, plot outlines, or character descriptions. Use voice notes to capture ideas on the go.

Study and Research: Organize study notes and research material. Use labels to categorize information by subject or topic.

Tips for Effective Use of Google Keep

Sync Across Devices: Ensure that your notes are synchronized across all your devices by using the same Google account. This allows you to access and edit your notes from anywhere.

Use Shortcuts: Familiarize yourself with Google Keep shortcuts to quickly create and manage notes. For example, press "C" to create a new note or "L" to create a new list on the web.

Integrate with Other Apps: Integrate Google Keep with other Google Workspace apps for enhanced productivity. For example, attach Keep notes to Google Docs for reference while writing or use Keep reminders in Google Calendar.

Regularly Review and Organize: Periodically review your notes to archive old ones, update tasks, and reorganize your labels. This keeps your Keep account clutter-free and efficient.

Utilize Voice Commands: On mobile devices, use voice commands to quickly create notes or set reminders. This is especially useful when you're on the go.

Adding Reminders to Notes

Step 1: Open Google Keep. Access Google Keep through your preferred method:

- **Web Browser:** Go to keep.google.com.
- **Mobile App:** Open the Google Keep app on your Android or iOS device.

Step 2: Create or open a note. Start a new note by clicking on the "Take a note" field or selecting an existing note that you want to add a reminder to.

Step 3: Click on the reminder icon. In the note toolbar, click on the reminder icon, which looks like a bell with a plus sign. On the mobile app, this icon is usually located at the bottom of the screen.

Step 4: Set the reminder. A menu will appear with options to set the reminder for a specific time or place:

- **Time-Based Reminders:** Choose a preset time like "Later today," "Tomorrow," or "Next week." For a custom time, click on "Pick date & time" and select the exact date and time you want the reminder.
- **Location-Based Reminders:** Select "Pick place" to set a location-based reminder. Enter the address or choose a place from the map. Google Keep will notify you when you arrive at the specified location.

Step 5: Save the reminder. Once you've set the desired time or location, click "Save." The reminder icon will appear on your note, indicating that a reminder has been set.

Managing Reminders

Step 1: View all reminders. To see all your reminders in one place, click on the "Reminders" tab on the left sidebar in the web version or the menu icon in the mobile app.

Step 2: Edit reminders. To edit a reminder, open the note with the reminder set. Click on the reminder icon, adjust the time or location, and save the changes.

Step 3: Delete reminders. To remove a reminder, open the note and click on the reminder icon. Select "Delete" to remove the reminder from the note.

Receiving Notifications

Step 1: Ensure notifications are enabled. Make sure notifications for Google Keep are enabled on your device. On mobile devices, go to your device settings, find Google Keep in the app list, and ensure notifications are turned on.

Step 2: Customize notification settings. On Android, you can customize notification settings such as sound, vibration, and priority. Go to your device settings, select "Apps & notifications," find Google Keep, and adjust the notification settings as needed.

Step 3: Receive reminders. At the set time or location, you will receive a notification on your device reminding you of the note. Tap on the notification to open the note in Google Keep.

Tips for Using Reminders and Notifications Effectively

Set Specific Times: When setting time-based reminders, choose specific times rather than vague periods to ensure you get notified at the most convenient moment.

Use Location-Based Reminders: Take advantage of location-based reminders for tasks that need to be completed at specific places, such as picking up groceries when you arrive at the store.

Combine Reminders with Labels: Organize your notes with labels and use reminders to prioritize tasks within those labels. This helps in managing tasks efficiently.

Review Reminders Regularly: Regularly review your reminders to update or delete those that are no longer relevant. This keeps your reminders list up to date and useful.

Synchronize Across Devices: Ensure you are signed in to the same Google account on all your devices to synchronize reminders and notifications. This allows you to receive reminders no matter which device you are using.

Google Gemini

Google Gemini is an advanced AI-driven platform developed by Google, designed to provide intelligent solutions for various industries. Leveraging machine learning, data analytics, and natural language processing, Google Gemini aims to transform how businesses operate by offering tailored insights, predictive analytics, and automation capabilities.

Key Features of Google Gemini

Advanced Analytics: Google Gemini offers powerful data analytics capabilities, enabling businesses to analyze large datasets quickly and efficiently. It uses machine learning algorithms to uncover patterns, trends, and insights that are not easily identifiable through traditional methods.

Predictive Analytics: With its predictive analytics feature, Google Gemini can forecast future trends and behaviors based on historical data. This helps businesses make informed decisions, anticipate market changes, and optimize strategies.

Natural Language Processing (NLP): Google Gemini's NLP capabilities allow it to understand and process human language. This feature is essential for applications such as chatbots, sentiment analysis, and automated customer support.

Automation: The platform automates repetitive and time-consuming tasks, freeing up human resources for more strategic activities. Automation can be applied to various processes, including data entry, reporting, and customer interactions.

Integration with Google Cloud: Google Gemini seamlessly integrates with Google Cloud services, providing robust infrastructure and security. This integration ensures that data is stored, processed, and managed in a secure and scalable environment.

Customization and Flexibility: Google Gemini can be customized to meet the specific needs of different industries. Businesses can tailor the platform's features and functionalities to align with their unique requirements and objectives.

Real-Time Insights: The platform provides real-time insights and analytics, enabling businesses to respond swiftly to emerging trends and opportunities. This real-time capability is crucial for maintaining a competitive edge in fast-paced markets.

User-Friendly Interface: Google Gemini features an intuitive and user-friendly interface, making it accessible to users with varying levels of technical expertise. The platform is designed to facilitate easy navigation and efficient use.

Uses of Google Gemini

Marketing and Sales: Google Gemini helps marketing and sales teams by providing insights into customer behavior, preferences, and trends. Predictive analytics can forecast sales, optimize marketing campaigns, and improve customer targeting.

Customer Support: With its NLP capabilities, Google Gemini can power intelligent chatbots and virtual assistants that provide efficient and accurate customer support. These AI-driven tools can handle a large volume of queries, reducing the workload on human agents.

Financial Services: In the financial sector, Google Gemini can be used for risk assessment, fraud detection, and investment analysis. Its advanced analytics help financial institutions make data-driven decisions and improve operational efficiency.

Healthcare: Google Gemini supports healthcare providers by analyzing patient data, predicting disease outbreaks, and optimizing treatment plans. The platform's real-time insights can enhance patient care and streamline healthcare operations.

Retail: Retail businesses can leverage Google Gemini for inventory management, demand forecasting, and personalized customer experiences. The platform's predictive analytics help retailers optimize stock levels and enhance customer satisfaction.

Manufacturing: In manufacturing, Google Gemini can optimize production processes, predict equipment failures, and improve supply chain management. The platform's automation capabilities reduce downtime and enhance operational efficiency.

Education: Educational institutions can use Google Gemini to analyze student performance, personalize learning experiences, and predict academic outcomes. The platform's data-driven insights help educators make informed decisions.

Logistics and Supply Chain: Google Gemini improves logistics and supply chain operations by optimizing routes, managing inventory, and predicting demand. Its real-time analytics enhance efficiency and reduce costs.

Human Resources: HR departments can benefit from Google Gemini by using it for talent acquisition, employee performance analysis, and workforce planning. The platform's predictive capabilities help in making strategic HR decisions.

Step 1: Access Google Gemini. Sign up for Google Gemini through the Google Cloud Platform. Ensure you have the necessary permissions and access rights.

Step 2: Integrate Data Sources. Connect your data sources to Google Gemini. This can include databases, cloud storage, and other data repositories. Ensure data is clean and properly formatted for analysis.

Step 3: Configure the Platform. Customize Google Gemini to align with your business needs. Set up dashboards, define key metrics, and configure alerts and notifications.

Step 4: Train the AI Models. Use historical data to train the machine learning models. Google Gemini's automated machine learning tools simplify this process, allowing you to build and deploy models quickly.

Step 5: Analyze and Act. Utilize the insights and recommendations provided by Google Gemini to make informed decisions. Regularly monitor the platform's outputs and adjust your strategies as needed.

Step 6: Scale and Optimize. As your business grows, scale your use of Google Gemini by integrating additional data sources and refining your AI models. Continuously optimize the platform's configurations to maximize its benefits.

How to Use Google Gemini with Google Tools

Google Gemini is designed to integrate seamlessly with various Google tools, enhancing your ability to harness AI-driven insights and automation across different applications.

Integrating Google Gemini with Google Workspace

Step 1: Access Google Gemini through Google Cloud. Sign in to your Google Cloud Platform account and navigate to Google Gemini. Ensure you have the appropriate permissions to access and use the service.

Step 2: Connect Google Workspace Apps. Integrate Google Gemini with Google Workspace apps such as Google Sheets, Google Docs, Google Calendar, and Gmail. This integration allows Gemini to analyze data from these sources and provide actionable insights.

Step 3: Use Google Sheets for Data Analysis. Import datasets into Google Sheets and use Google Gemini to perform advanced data analysis. Gemini can help identify patterns, trends, and correlations within your data, making it easier to derive meaningful insights.

Step 4: Enhance Google Docs with AI Insights. When working on documents, use Google Gemini to insert data-driven insights, summaries, and recommendations directly into your Google Docs. This feature is particularly useful for creating reports, proposals, and strategic plans.

Step 5: Schedule and Automate Tasks with Google Calendar. Use Google Gemini to analyze your calendar data and optimize scheduling. Gemini can suggest the best times for meetings, predict potential conflicts, and even automate the scheduling of recurring tasks.

Step 6: Optimize Email Communication with Gmail. Integrate Google Gemini with Gmail to enhance email communication. Gemini can analyze email content, suggest responses, prioritize emails, and automate follow-up reminders.

Utilizing Google Gemini with Google Analytics

Step 1: Link Google Analytics with Google Gemini. Connect your Google Analytics account to Google Gemini to access web traffic data and user behavior insights.

Step 2: Analyze Website Performance. Use Google Gemini to analyze website performance metrics such as page views, bounce rates, and conversion rates. Gemini's advanced analytics can identify trends and suggest optimizations to improve user engagement.

Step 3: Personalize User Experience. Leverage the insights from Google Gemini to personalize user experiences on your website. Implement changes based on data-driven recommendations to enhance user satisfaction and increase conversions.

Leveraging Google Gemini with Google Ads

Step 1: Integrate Google Ads with Google Gemini. Connect your Google Ads account to Google Gemini to analyze ad performance data.

Step 2: Optimize Ad Campaigns. Use Google Gemini to analyze the effectiveness of your ad campaigns. Gemini can provide insights into click-through rates, conversion rates, and return on investment (ROI), helping you optimize your ad spend.

Step 3: Automate Ad Adjustments. Set up automation rules in Google Ads based on recommendations from Google Gemini. Automate bid adjustments, ad placements, and targeting parameters to maximize the efficiency of your ad campaigns.

Enhancing Google Cloud Services with Google Gemini

Step 1: Use Google Cloud Storage with Google Gemini. Store and manage large datasets in Google Cloud Storage and use Google Gemini to analyze and derive insights from these datasets.

Step 2: Implement Machine Learning Models. Deploy machine learning models developed in Google Gemini on Google Cloud AI Platform. This allows you to leverage powerful AI capabilities for predictive analytics, image recognition, natural language processing, and more.

Step 3: Automate Cloud Functions. Integrate Google Gemini with Google Cloud Functions to automate various cloud operations. Set up triggers and workflows based on insights and recommendations from Gemini.

By integrating Google Gemini with various Google tools, you can create a cohesive and efficient workflow that leverages AI-driven insights and automation to enhance productivity, decision-making, and strategic planning.

Chatting with Gemini

Chatting with Google Gemini allows users to interact with the AI in natural language, making it easier to obtain insights, perform tasks, and automate processes.

Differences Between Gemini and Gemini Advanced

Google Gemini:

- **Basic Features:** Google Gemini offers core AI functionalities, including basic data analysis, natural language processing, and automation capabilities.

- **User Interface:** The interface is designed to be user-friendly and accessible to users with varying levels of technical expertise.
- **Integration:** Seamlessly integrates with Google Workspace apps and other Google services, providing essential tools for productivity and collaboration.
- **Scalability:** Suitable for small to medium-sized businesses that need basic AI-driven solutions.

Google Gemini Advanced:

- **Enhanced Features:** Google Gemini Advanced includes all the features of the basic version, plus advanced analytics, deeper machine learning capabilities, and enhanced customization options.
- **User Interface:** The advanced interface includes additional tools and options for more complex tasks and deeper insights.
- **Integration:** Offers extended integration capabilities with more third-party applications and advanced Google Cloud services.
- **Scalability:** Ideal for large enterprises that require sophisticated AI-driven solutions for complex data analysis and automation.

Additional Tips

Customize Your Experience: Tailor Google Gemini to meet your specific needs by customizing its features and settings. This ensures you get the most relevant and actionable insights for your business.

Regularly Update Data: Ensure that your data sources are regularly updated and maintained. Accurate and up-to-date data is crucial for obtaining reliable insights from Google Gemini.

Use Templates and Pre-Built Models: Take advantage of templates and pre-built machine learning models provided by Google Gemini. These can help you get started quickly and efficiently with common use cases.

Collaborate with Team Members: Use Google Gemini's collaboration features to work with team members on data analysis, project planning, and decision-making. Sharing insights and working together enhances productivity and ensures everyone is aligned.

Leverage Training and Support: Utilize Google's training resources and support services to enhance your understanding and use of Google Gemini. Continuous learning ensures you stay updated with the latest features and best practices.

Security & Compliance

Ensuring security and compliance is critical for any organization using digital tools and services. Google Workspace provides a robust set of features to help maintain high levels of security and meet compliance requirements. This section covers essential aspects like Google Authenticator, user roles and permissions, two-factor authentication, compliance and certification, and auditing and monitoring.

Google Authenticator

Google Authenticator is a two-factor authentication (2FA) application that provides an additional layer of security by generating time-based one-time passwords (TOTP). Here's how to set it up and use it.

Setting Up Authenticator

Step 1: Download the Google Authenticator app. Visit the Google Play Store (Android) or Apple App Store (iOS) and download the Google Authenticator app.

Step 2: Sign in to your Google account. Go to your Google Account settings on your web browser by visiting myaccount.google.com and sign in.

Step 3: Navigate to the Security section. In your Google Account settings, click on the "Security" tab.

Step 4: Set up 2-Step Verification. Under "Signing in to Google," find "2-Step Verification" and click on it. Follow the on-screen instructions to set up 2-Step Verification.

Step 5: Select Authenticator App. During the setup process, you will be prompted to choose your second step. Select "Authenticator app" and follow the instructions.

Step 6: Scan the QR code. Open the Google Authenticator app on your mobile device, tap the plus icon (+) to add a new account, and scan the QR code displayed on your computer screen.

Step 7: Enter the code. The Google Authenticator app will generate a six-digit code. Enter this code on your computer to complete the setup.

Step 8: Backup codes. Google will provide backup codes that you can use if you lose access to your mobile device. Save these codes in a secure location.

Using Google Authenticator

Step 1: Sign in to your Google account. Enter your username and password as usual.

Step 2: Open the Google Authenticator app. On your mobile device, open the app to retrieve the six-digit code.

Step 3: Enter the code. Enter the code generated by Google Authenticator to complete the sign-in process. Remember, the code changes every 30 seconds, so use the most current one.

User Roles and Permissions

Managing user roles and permissions in Google Workspace ensures that users have appropriate access levels and can perform their tasks without compromising security.

Managing User Roles and Permissions

Step 1: Sign in to the Google Admin console. Go to admin.google.com and sign in with your administrator account.

Step 2: Navigate to the Users section. In the Admin console, click on "Users" to view the list of all users in your organization.

Step 3: Select a user. Click on the name of the user whose roles and permissions you want to manage.

Step 4: Assign roles. Under the user details, find the "Roles and Privileges" section. Click "Assign roles" to open the role assignment settings.

Step 5: Choose a role. Select the appropriate role for the user (e.g., Super Admin, Groups Admin, User Management Admin). You can assign multiple roles if necessary.

Step 6: Save changes. Click "Save" to apply the changes. The user will now have the permissions associated with the assigned role.

Step 7: Create custom roles (optional). If default roles do not meet your needs, you can create custom roles. Go to "Roles" in the Admin console, click "Create new role," define the role's permissions, and assign it to users as needed.

Two-Factor Authentication (2FA)

Two-factor authentication (2FA) adds an extra layer of security by requiring a second form of verification in addition to a password.

Enforcing 2FA

Step 1: Sign in to the Google Admin console. Go to admin.google.com and sign in with your administrator account.

Step 2: Navigate to Security settings. In the Admin console, click on "Security" to access security settings.

Step 3: Set up 2-Step Verification. Under "Security," click on "2-Step Verification" and then "Set up."

Step 4: Enforce 2FA for users. In the 2-Step Verification settings, click on "Enforcement" and choose the enforcement level (e.g., enforce for all users or specific organizational units).

Step 5: Notify users. Inform your users about the requirement to set up 2FA and provide them with instructions on how to configure their second step (e.g., using Google Authenticator, SMS, or backup codes).

Step 6: Monitor compliance. Use the Admin console to monitor which users have set up 2FA and follow up with those who have not yet completed the process.

Compliance and Certification

Google Workspace is designed to help organizations meet various compliance and certification standards.

Key Compliance and Certification Features

Data Protection: Google Workspace ensures data protection through encryption, data loss prevention (DLP), and advanced threat protection.

Regulatory Compliance: Google Workspace complies with major regulations such as GDPR, HIPAA, and FERPA. It provides tools to help organizations manage compliance requirements.

Certification: Google Workspace holds certifications such as ISO/IEC 27001, 27017, 27018, SOC 1/2/3, and FedRAMP, which attest to its robust security and compliance measures.

Auditing and Monitoring

Auditing and monitoring are crucial for maintaining security and ensuring compliance. Google Workspace provides comprehensive tools for auditing user activity and monitoring security events.

Step-by-Step Procedure for Auditing and Monitoring

Step 1: Sign in to the Google Admin console. Go to admin.google.com and sign in with your administrator account.

Step 2: Access the Security dashboard. In the Admin console, click on "Security" to open the security dashboard.

Step 3: View security reports. Under the "Security" section, click on "Reports" to access various security reports. These reports provide insights into user activity, login attempts, and potential security threats.

Step 4: Set up alerts. Go to the "Alert Center" in the Security dashboard to set up alerts for specific activities, such as suspicious login attempts or data breaches. Configure the alert settings to notify administrators via email or SMS.

Step 5: Review audit logs. Click on "Audit" in the Security dashboard to view detailed logs of user activity, including file sharing, login attempts, and admin actions. Use filters to narrow down the logs and focus on specific events.

Step 6: Investigate incidents. If an alert or audit log indicates a potential security incident, investigate the details and take appropriate actions, such as resetting passwords, revoking access, or contacting affected users.

Step 7: Regularly review security settings. Periodically review and update your security settings to ensure they align with best practices and address any new threats or compliance requirements.

Financial & Transactional Tools

Google offers several financial and transactional tools to streamline payment processes, manage business transactions, and stay updated on financial markets. This section covers how to set up and use Google Pay, get started with Google Merchant Center, and use Google Finance effectively.

Google Pay

Google Pay is a digital wallet platform and online payment system developed by Google to power in-app and tap-to-pay purchases on mobile devices, enabling users to make payments with Android phones, tablets, or watches.

Setting Up Google Pay

Step 1: Download the Google Pay app. Visit the Google Play Store (Android) or Apple App Store (iOS) and download the Google Pay app.

Step 2: Open the Google Pay app. Tap on the Google Pay app icon to open it.

Step 3: Sign in to your Google account. Use your Google account credentials to sign in.

Step 4: Add a payment method. Tap on the "Payment methods" section and then tap on "Add payment method." You can add a credit card, debit card, or link your bank account.

Step 5: Enter your card details. Follow the prompts to enter your card number, expiration date, CVV, and billing address. For bank accounts, enter your bank details as instructed.

Step 6: Verify your payment method. Depending on your card issuer or bank, you may need to verify your payment method. This can be done through a verification code sent via SMS, email, or a phone call.

Step 7: Set up security. Enable fingerprint, face recognition, or PIN authentication for added security when making payments.

Step 8: Complete the setup. Once verified, your payment method will be added to Google Pay, and you can start using it for transactions.

Step 1: Open the Google Pay app. Tap on the Google Pay app icon to open it.

Step 2: Choose the payment method. If you have multiple payment methods, select the one you want to use for the transaction.

Step 3: Make a payment. For in-store payments, hold your phone near the contactless payment terminal and wait for the confirmation. For in-app or online purchases, select Google Pay as your payment option and follow the prompts.

Step 4: Confirm the transaction. Use your preferred authentication method (fingerprint, face recognition, or PIN) to confirm the transaction.

Step 5: Receive confirmation. Once the payment is processed, you will receive a confirmation notification on your device.

Google Merchant Center

Google Merchant Center is a tool that helps you upload your store and product data to Google and make it available for Google Shopping and other Google services.

How to Get Started with Google Merchant Center

Step 1: Sign in to Google Merchant Center. Visit merchants.google.com and sign in with your Google account.

Step 2: Set up your Merchant Center account. Follow the prompts to enter your business information, such as your business name, website URL, and contact information.

Step 3: Verify your website. Google will ask you to verify that you own the website you entered. You can do this by adding an HTML file to your website, adding an HTML tag, using Google Analytics, or using Google Tag Manager.

Step 4: Configure your settings. In the Merchant Center dashboard, go to "Settings" and configure your tax and shipping settings according to your business needs.

Step 5: Upload your product data. Create a product feed by going to the "Products" tab and selecting "Feeds." Follow the instructions to upload your product data. You can do this manually, through a scheduled fetch, or by using a third-party platform.

Step 6: Review and submit your feed. Once your product data is uploaded, review it for accuracy. Submit your feed for approval by Google.

Step 7: Monitor your feed. Regularly check the "Diagnostics" tab to ensure your product data remains compliant with Google's policies and guidelines.

Google Finance

Google Finance provides up-to-date information on financial markets, stocks, and economic news. It is a useful tool for investors, traders, and anyone interested in financial data.

How to Use Google Finance

Step 1: Access Google Finance. Go to finance.google.com in your web browser.

Step 2: Search for a stock or financial instrument. Use the search bar at the top of the page to enter the name or ticker symbol of the stock or financial instrument you want to track.

Step 3: View detailed information. Click on the search result to view detailed information, including the current price, historical data, news, and analysis.

Step 4: Create a watchlist. Click on the "Watchlist" tab and add stocks or financial instruments you want to monitor. You can create multiple watchlists to organize your investments.

Step 5: Set up alerts. Go to the "Alerts" section and set up price alerts for stocks or financial instruments. You will receive notifications when the price reaches your specified threshold.

Step 6: Analyze financial data. Use the charts and analysis tools available on Google Finance to study price trends, compare different stocks, and make informed investment decisions.

DAILY TOOLS

Google offers a variety of daily tools that can help streamline everyday activities, from navigation to entertainment and shopping. This section covers how to use Google Maps, Google Lens, Google TV, and the Google Play Store, along with their key features and examples of usage.

Google Maps

Google Maps is a comprehensive mapping service that provides directions, real-time traffic updates, local business information, and much more.

How to Use Google Maps

Step 1: Open Google Maps. Access Google Maps on your web browser by visiting maps.google.com or open the Google Maps app on your mobile device.

Step 2: Sign in to your Google account. While not necessary, signing in allows you to save locations, see past searches, and access personalized recommendations.

Step 3: Search for a location. Use the search bar at the top to enter the name or address of the location you want to find. Press Enter or tap the search icon.

Step 4: Get directions. Click or tap on the "Directions" button. Enter your starting point and destination. Choose your mode of transport (car, public transit, walking, or biking).

Step 5: View route details. Google Maps will show you the route options along with estimated travel times. Select the preferred route to see step-by-step directions.

Step 6: Explore nearby. Use the "Explore" tab to find nearby restaurants, gas stations, attractions, and other points of interest.

Step 7: Save locations. Click on a location and select "Save" to add it to your saved places, such as "Favorites" or "Want to go."

Step 8: Share your location. Tap on the blue dot representing your current location, then tap "Share your location" to send your real-time location to others.

Step 9: Use Street View. Drag the yellow Pegman icon to a location on the map to view street-level imagery.

Google Lens

Google Lens is a powerful image recognition tool that allows you to search for information, translate text, and interact with the world around you using your camera.

How to Use Google Lens

Step 1: Open Google Lens. Access Google Lens via the Google app, Google Photos, or the Google Lens app on your mobile device.

Step 2: Use your camera. Point your camera at an object, text, or scene you want to learn more about. Tap the Lens icon.

Step 3: Capture the image. Tap the shutter button to capture the image or select an image from your gallery.

Step 4: Analyze the image. Google Lens will analyze the image and provide information, such as identifying objects, translating text, or showing similar items.

Step 5: Interact with results. Tap on the results to explore more about what you captured. For example, you can visit websites, view product details, or read reviews.

Examples of Google Lens Usage

Identify Plants and Animals: Point Google Lens at a plant or animal to identify it and learn more about it.

Translate Text: Use Google Lens to translate text in real-time. Point the camera at the text and select the "Translate" option.

Shopping: Find similar products by pointing Google Lens at an item. It will show you where you can buy it online.

Explore Landmarks: Point Google Lens at a landmark to learn about its history, opening hours, and other relevant information.

Scan QR Codes: Use Google Lens to scan QR codes for quick access to websites, menus, or other information.

Google TV

Google TV integrates streaming services, live TV, and apps into one platform, providing a seamless entertainment experience. Here's how to use Google TV.

How to Use Google TV

Step 1: Set up your Google TV. Connect your Google TV device to your TV and follow the on-screen instructions to complete the setup.

Step 2: Sign in to your Google account. Use your Google account to sign in and access personalized recommendations and saved content.

Step 3: Explore the home screen. The home screen displays recommended content from various streaming services based on your viewing history.

Step 4: Search for content. Use the search bar or voice search to find movies, TV shows, apps, and more.

Step 5: Install apps. Navigate to the "Apps" tab to browse and install streaming services and other apps.

Step 6: Watch live TV. If you have a compatible live TV service, integrate it with Google TV to access live channels from the home screen.

Step 7: Manage your watchlist. Add shows and movies to your watchlist by selecting the "Add to Watchlist" option.

Step 8: Use the Google Assistant. Press the Google Assistant button on your remote to search for content, control smart home devices, and ask questions.

Google Play Store

The Google Play Store is the official app store for Android devices, offering apps, games, books, movies, and more. Here's how to use the Google Play Store.

How to Use the Google Play Store

Step 1: Open the Google Play Store. Access the Play Store on your Android device by tapping the Play Store icon.

Step 2: Sign in to your Google account. Sign in with your Google account to download and purchase apps and content.

Step 3: Browse categories. Use the tabs at the bottom to browse different categories such as Apps, Games, Movies & TV, and Books.

Step 4: Search for content. Use the search bar at the top to find specific apps, games, movies, or books.

Step 5: Download or purchase. Tap on the content you want, then tap "Install" or "Buy" to download or purchase it. Follow the prompts to complete the transaction.

Step 6: Manage your apps. Go to "My apps & games" in the menu to update, uninstall, or manage your apps.

Step 7: Redeem gift cards. Tap on the menu icon, select "Redeem," and enter the code from your Google Play gift card.

Step 8: Enable parental controls. Go to "Settings" and enable parental controls to restrict content based on age ratings.

Features of the Google Play Store

App and Game Downloads: Access millions of apps and games across various categories.

Content Recommendations: Personalized recommendations based on your preferences and usage history.

Secure Transactions: Safe and secure payment options for purchasing apps, games, and other content.

Parental Controls: Tools to manage and restrict content for children.

Updates and Notifications: Regular updates for apps and notifications for new content and offers.

Conclusion

In an era where digital tools and technologies are constantly evolving, mastering the wide array of applications and platforms offered by Google can significantly enhance your productivity, efficiency, and overall digital experience. From managing daily tasks with Google Workspace to leveraging advanced analytics with Google Gemini, and optimizing your daily life with tools like Google Maps, Google Lens, Google TV, and Google Play Store, the possibilities are endless.

Throughout this guide, we have explored various features, step-by-step processes, and practical tips to help you make the most of these powerful tools. Whether you are a business professional looking to streamline operations, an educator seeking to enhance remote learning, or an individual aiming to improve personal productivity and entertainment, Google's suite of applications offers tailored solutions to meet your needs.

By integrating these tools into your daily routine, you can unlock new levels of efficiency and creativity, staying ahead in a fast-paced digital world. Embrace these technologies, continue exploring their capabilities, and remain curious about new updates and features that Google regularly introduces.

Remember, the key to maximizing the benefits of these tools lies in continuous learning and adaptation. Stay informed, practice regularly, and do not hesitate to experiment with different functionalities to find what works best for you. As you grow more comfortable and proficient with these applications, you will find yourself navigating the digital landscape with greater confidence and ease.